NEVER FAR
FROM HOME

D1714836

CINDY BARNETT

Printed in the United States of America

Publishing services by Selah Publishing Group, LLC, Arizona. The views expressed or implied in this work do not necessarily reflect those of Selah Publishing Group.

ISBN: 1-58930-162-5
Library of Congress Control Number:2005907750

Dedicated to my children—

So you will know why we are the way we are

PART 1

CHAPTER 1

Whether I shall turn out to be the hero of my own life,
or whether that station will be held by anybody else, these
pages must show.
CHARLES DICKENS—DAVID COPPERFIELD

They say you can't go back home again. You can't go back in time, and you can't go back to the scene of your childhood and find it unchanged. Places change, and people change. My sister, Mindy, and I did try to go there one day, to the house our dad had built onto the back of The Old Dutch Mill Service Center. We parked the car on the crumbling cement where gas pumps had once stood and climbed over piles of wood and trash to reach our childhood home. Of course, it seemed much smaller to our older eyes. Nothing seemed the same.

We looked through gaps in the wall, for the roof had caved in, and we could see right inside. We saw the limestone that used to be our fireplace, where we had posed for pictures in pajamas and slippers. We saw the three little windows on the front door and some faded knotty pine. We didn't stay long and kept looking over our shoulders for fear someone would think we were trespassing, but how could we be trespassing on what used to be ours, our whole little world? The home we remember can only be visited in the imagination, but I will try to take you there.

There was a time when The Old Dutch Mill was the center of life in Disko, Indiana. Disko was little more than a collection of houses, two or three stores, and a post office, just off a bend in the road between Akron and North Manchester in northern Indiana. The spelling of *Disko* was a matter of debate; the signs read *Disko* coming in and *Disco* going out. Right on that bend in the road sat The Old Dutch Mill, a general store and filling station run by my parents, Donald and Eileen Gearhart.

It was shaped like a Dutch windmill without the giant wind paddles, almost like a lighthouse, with a curved-out wall at the front of the store. It was white with dark shingles in a band around the top. Connected to it was a garage, where my dad was the mechanic. A sign with the flying horse Pegasus hung high by the road, advertising Mobil gas. The front of the store displayed red Coca-Cola signs and a big round clock. Approaching Disko from either direction, a person would see billboards my dad had built declaring, "Buy! For less! Old Dutch Mill Service Center. Groceries, Gas, Pop."

Inside the store, the shelves were filled with groceries, cosmetics, toys, clothing, candy, hardware, and just about anything else a person might need. If you wanted a bottle of pop, you would open the Coca-Cola cooler, take the bottle, dripping wet, out of the chilled water, and open it with the can opener built right into the side. You could buy fresh meat and cheese there, too. The meat cooler was filled with long rolls of Longhorn Colby cheese and varieties of Eckrich cold meat. Inside the freezer were Sealtest ice-cream bars, fudgesickles, and other frozen treats. Only name brands like Eckrich and Sealtest were sold at The Dutch Mill. Don would slice meat onto the scales using the Hobart meat slicer, wrap it in white paper, and tie it up with string. If you wanted a sandwich or a malted milkshake, they had that, too. You could sit on a stool and eat at the counter, and sometimes on weekends they would play music and you could dance. Although I didn't think about it at the time, The Dutch Mill was an extraordinary place to grow up.

Don and his brother Leo had opened this store after they returned from Europe at the end of World War II. Don had been drafted into the army four years earlier and was sent to Panama to work with pack mules and cargo ships around the Panama Canal. Later he went to England, then on to Germany, where he served under General Patton in the Battle of the Bulge. He was a mechanic, working on trucks and artillery in the Third Artillery Battalion and was part of the American army that moved in to occupy Germany. Leo had served in the army in Italy.

America was optimistic after World War II, and soon Dwight Eisenhower was president in a time of peace and prosperity. People were getting married and starting families. It was the Baby Boom. Men were going into business, and life was getting back to normal. People in Disko liked to come to the store where these two soldier brothers would joke with them and they could have a good time.

Don soon met and fell in love with a pretty lady who lived just down the street behind The Dutch Mill. Her name was Eileen Bowers. She had a round face with slightly full lips and a cheery friendliness that drew him in. Her dresses were fitted around the waist, showing off her slim figure. Eileen was divorced, living with her mother and two children after her husband, Ralph Bowers, had deserted her. Ralph had gone to New Orleans saying he would come back soon, but he never did, leaving her with her six-year-old son, Mickey Jo, and a twelve-year-old daughter, Greta Elaine. As I looked through the box of family pictures years later, I often came upon the photo of Ralph, a good-looking young man in a sailor uniform.

Eileen and Donald got married and lived above the store in the windmill tower. Donald was thirty, and Eileen was thirty-two. I was born about three years later, on February 25, 1952. Had I been a boy, my name would have been Donald Patrick.

Aunt Opal, Dad's sister, sent a congratulation card to Mom with a note saying, "Hope this note finds you and the girl doing okay. I hope, too, Donald isn't so disappointed because he had his heart set on a boy. He will love a little daughter just as well. Suppose he'll have to order a boy later."

Well, he didn't get a boy, just two girls. My sister, Mindy Ellen, was born two years later, on September 20, 1954, and Donald loved his little girls dearly. He called us his little Pidgie Widgies. We kissed him on his cheek before we went to bed every night, his rough, dry skin smelling like cigars or cigarettes, and we affectionately called him "Daddy" as long as he lived.

Daddy built a house onto the back of the store for his growing family with little more than common sense and ingenuity. He made it out of cement blocks with a flat roof. The plumbing ran exposed along the inside of the outer walls, so he built a long wooden couch to cover the pipes, and Mom sewed big cushions to make it soft. The floors were covered with tiles in a checkerboard pattern, and all the walls were beautiful knotty pine. A limestone fireplace with a gas log was at one end of the living room. This cement-block house may have seemed a little plain on the outside, but I thought it was beautiful and homey on the inside.

Daddy designed and built all the kitchen cupboards from knotty pine, as well as custom shelves, couches, cubbyholes, a laundry chute, and secret playrooms. Our dining-room table was built into the wall exactly like a restaurant booth. A sliding door separated the house from the store.

Outside we had yard options in all directions. Our side yard, which seemed to me the size of a football field, was the center for neighborhood sports with its baseball diamond, basketball court, and pole-vault pit. We called it "down over the hill" because the whole yard was a few feet lower than The Dutch Mill and the road. In the center of this yard was a clump of bushes, good for a hideout, and along the side of the yard and behind the house were elm trees planted in rows. At the far end of the sports yard were the tallest trees, only a few feet wide, like giant skinny soldiers marking our property line.

The narrow back yard was rubbed bare where Nip, our black dog with curly white spots on his chest, was chained to his doghouse. He guarded the house and tended to bite strangers. When we looked through *The Little Golden Book of Dogs*, I asked Mom what kind of dog Nip was. She flipped past the collies and Labradors to the last page, the mongrel. It didn't look like Nip, but Mom said, "Nip's a mongrel. He's just a mixture of all kinds of dogs."

Beyond the elm trees behind the house, a field planted in soybeans or corn stretched to a farmhouse a quarter mile away. A white birch tree, with paper-thin curls of bark, grew near the front of the store, and a silvery cottonwood tree, which Daddy had planted there for my mom, rustled outside my bedroom window. It was a wonderful place to grow up.

Daddy was my hero. He was dark-skinned and handsome with upper arms that bulged with muscles and a trim waist. He wore a cap over his closely trimmed hair. I thought he looked like James Arness, who played Matt Dillon in *Gunsmoke*. He had brown eyes, just like mine, and his sturdy workingman's hands had the same square palms as my little hands. He always wore traditional work outfits ordered from the catalog. He wore blue for a few years, then gray, then khaki.

I was proud of my dad. I felt safe and secure around him because he was confident and never seemed to worry. He was always working, always thinking of new projects to do. He dreamed and made plans. He wasn't a perfectionist, but he could get the job done. Though he was quiet, I always knew he loved me, and we understood each other perfectly—because I was quiet like him.

Mom surrounded us like the air, as familiar as our own faces, doing things for us, making everything work together smoothly. She was a 1950s stay-at-home mom, cooking meals from scratch that included all the food groups. She made the dresses we wore to school every day, and she took us every place we needed to go. She belonged to a homemakers' club and the Disko Methodist church. And she was smart. In school she had been at the top of her class and won awards for her speedy typing. She helped Daddy in the store and did all the bookkeeping for our home and the business.

Mom was a singer, singing to me as she put me to bed.

I love you
A bushel and a peck,
A bushel and a peck
And a hug around the neck.

Mindy and I played together constantly as little girls, even though I was a tomboy and Mindy liked to play with dolls. She was sensitive, artistic, more emotional, and more caring than I was. Because I was older and stronger, I sometimes teased and bullied her, or ignored her altogether. Our brother, Mick, was eight years older, and Elaine was fourteen years older than we were. Elaine helped care for me as a baby while my mom worked in the store, but before I was old enough to remember, Elaine had already graduated, married, had a baby, and moved out of our house. Mick, whom I always called Mike, only wanted to play with the other boys in town, so Mindy was my constant playmate.

We were children of the 1950s, when cowboys were popular with everyone. I was outfitted with complete cowboy duds, guns in holsters, fringed shirts and chaps, hats, and boots. Thinking I was a cowboy, I rode up and down the aisles of the store on my tricycle. Someone asked, "Who are you, little girl?"

I answered, "I'm Kit Carson."

Our favorite toys were our miniature cowboys and Indians. The plastic figures were forever fighting, the Indians with raised bows and arrows and the cowboys with guns. Some of the horses could be set back on their tails like they were rearing up, pawing the air. We even had a little metal frontier town with swinging saloon doors. We played with our cowboys and Indians by the hour in the house, or better yet, outside in the dirt.

Even our favorite TV shows were the westerns—*Roy Rogers*, *The Lone Ranger*, *Gunsmoke*, and *Bonanza*. As little girls, we had one of those plastic horses on springs. When it wore out, we cut out the saddle part and used it on our "fence horses." We bent over the top of the wire-mesh fence that connected the closely spaced elm trees in the back yard. Then we piled on blankets, saddlebags, and our plastic saddle, tied the reins around the trees, and rode the horses! We rode along, always in single file, feeling like we were real cowboys. If we wanted to gallop along and actually go somewhere, we used stick horses, with or without heads.

Mindy and I used our imagination to become whatever characters we wanted to be, from soldiers to moms. We started a library, making Mom check out our books, and opened a bank, with Mom having to open an account with us and write checks. I loved playing school, carrying around Mike's high-school algebra books and pretending I was doing homework. We dressed up in shorts and bathrobes to become boxers when Daddy watched the Monday night fights on TV. We had our own variety shows and acted out plays with Mom and Daddy as our whole audience. We played store and hospital in the junk room. We stocked our pretend store shelves with colored wooden blocks and discarded boxes of Jello or other items from the real store. We played hospital with Mindy's dolls.

Like most families in the 1950s, we bought a TV. The programs were in black and white, sometimes grainy or with lines flipping through the picture, but it was still the golden age of TV. The shows were clean, the good guys won, the families were ideal. Our TV was placed on a deep shelf at one end of the living room, about four feet from the floor. It was like being at the movies, only the screen was smaller, about nineteen-inches wide. Every evening our family sat together, with Daddy in his favorite tan chair, around the bluish glow of our TV. We watched programs like *Lassie*, *I Love Lucy*, *The Honeymooners*, *The Ed Sullivan Show*, *Superman*, *Leave It to Beaver*, and *The Howdy-Doody Show*. And, of course, the westerns, which Daddy loved.

Mom's mother, Lena McQuiston, lived just down the road behind The Old Dutch Mill. Grandma McQuiston was thin with bony hands and a wrinkly face. She always wore a dress unless she was working in the garden and then she wore blue jeans. My Grandpa, Roscoe McQuiston, was a round, jolly-looking man, like Santa Claus without a beard. In photographs he stands beside me, smiling with big cheeks and twinkly eyes, but I don't remember him at all. Mom said he went crazy after he was laid off from the railroad where he had worked his whole life. He didn't know what to do, so he walked up and down the railroad tracks, just disturbed and confused. Eventually they had to put him in the mental hospital. He lost weight and never got better.

Grandma would visit him in the hospital and showed me a picture of him with a crazy smile on his face, wearing baggy pants held on with a rope. Mom didn't like the picture. She said, "I don't like that picture, and I don't know why Grandma shows it to people. I just want to remember him the way he was."

Grandma's name was Lena Moore before she married Roscoe. Her mother was Cora Alma Thompson, and her father was Walter Scott Moore. Roscoe McQuiston's parents were William McQuiston and Eva McWilliams. Both Grandma and Grandpa had several brothers and sisters who lived around the Kokomo area, but my mom, whose full name was Gretchen Eileen McQuiston, grew up as an only child. She had a sister, Thelma Lenora, who only lived four months.

After Grandpa Roscoe died, Grandma was lonely living by herself, so I often stayed overnight with her to keep her company. In the winter, Grandma's house smelled faintly like kerosene from the big brown heater in her living room. The kitchen was white and cheerful. Many times I sat at the white enamel kitchen table with the black lines around the edge to eat my breakfast, staring out the window at the neighbor's tree limbs. I ate Special

K, Grandma's favorite cereal, out of white bowls decorated with cowboys on horses galloping around the edge. Sometimes she made big fluffy omelets that she called "egg pancakes." She had two cups with little figures sitting up in the bottom of them, one with a cat and one with a dog. I drank milk out of these cups, drinking it all so I could see the animal in the bottom.

The only song I remember Grandma singing was an old folk song, "The Poor Babes in the Woods," which she sang in a wavy, crackly voice. It gave Mindy and me the chills.

> My dear, do you know how a long time ago,
> Two poor little children whose names I don't know,
> Were stolen away on a bright summer's day,
> And left in the woods, so I've heard people say?
>
> And when it was night, how sad was their plight;
> The sun it went down, and the moon gave no light.
> They sobbed and they sighed, and they bitterly cried,
> Then the poor little things, they lay down and died.
>
> And when it was night, the robin so red
> Brought strawberry leaves and over them spread,
> And all the night long they sang them this song:
> "Poor babes in the wood, poor babes in the wood."

Grandma had boxes of puzzles that we put together in the evenings. We would choose a puzzle, usually some type of scenery, put it on a card table in the living room, and eat apple wedges, Ritz crackers, and pieces of cheese. We spent many evenings together like this before going upstairs to bed. She had two rooms upstairs—one was the bedroom and the other room was full of boxes.

Mom always said, "Your grandma is like most old people. They don't throw anything away. They just save it and store it in boxes." She said it was because they had lived through the Depression.

Mindy and I liked staying at Grandma's house, but sometimes she would get grouchy if we didn't obey and come after us with a yardstick.

In the summer, Mindy and I played outside under the big maple trees in Grandma's back yard. We climbed onto the low branches or played in the dirt around the tree roots. Behind the trees was a long shed, and beyond that was a terraced hill full of flowers leading down to a stone fireplace and a cement seat shaped like a toadstool. Mindy and I imagined fantasy worlds full of little creatures underneath the grass and around the tree roots.

Grandma loved flowers, and she filled her yards and gardens with them. Even the vegetable garden had more flowers than vegetables. Row after row of colorful gladioli leaned this way and that. In the fall she dug up the glad bulbs, which looked like little gold or maroon cookies, to store them for winter. I helped her carefully peel off the outer layer of the bulbs, arrange them on trays, and slide them onto shelves in the basement, like so many cookie sheets going into the oven. She took pride in her flowers and yard. If she saw a mole daring to dig tunnels in her beautiful yard or garden, she'd go after it with a pitchfork, sneaking up while it was digging and then giving it a jab.

Mom would occasionally take us to Kokomo so we could visit Grandma's sister Inez. Inez and Grandma were best friends, as long as they kept their distance and just wrote letters and visited occasionally.

Sometimes Grandma wanted me to write a letter to Aunt Inez. She would say, "Inez would be tickled to death to get a letter from you." So I would fill a page or two of stationery with squiggly lines, and she sent my letter along with hers.

Inez lived in a small wood-frame house in a row of crowded houses just off busy Markland Avenue in Kokomo. She was always glad to see us, hugging us close to her soft, bulgy body. Her house was full of a variety of furniture, trinkets, and boxes of stored things. Aunt Alice also lived in Kokomo, and her house was the same. Alice had straight bobbed hair, was thin like Grandma, and always seemed a little wild-looking. Inez and Alice were much worse than Grandma about filling rooms with boxes.

Inez had a brown dog named Poody who was round as a barrel. He lived in the house with her, almost like another person. Inez was a Christian, although her spiritual instruction came primarily from religious TV programs and magazines. She always spoke of hoping and praying concerning everything.

Visiting Aunt Inez in Kokomo was our first experience with city life. I think Mom and Daddy were afraid of cities, so we never went to Indianapolis and wouldn't think of going to Chicago. It was in Kokomo that we saw a new store idea, stores connected together called a "mall," and we visited one of the new fast-food places called Burger Chef. When we saw the road construction on US 31, Mom said they were building a new system of super highways across the country that would have loops of road like four-leaf clovers instead of intersections. Cars wouldn't even have to stop. But overall, we didn't like the noisy, ugly city life that we saw around Markland Avenue.

CHAPTER 2

As a little girl, I loved books and learning. Mom read stories to me from a set of books by *Better Homes and Gardens*, a book each of fairy tales, bedtime stories, adventure stories, nursery rhymes, and animal stories. She would read stories such as "Jack and the Beanstalk" while I looked at the pictures. She also taught me how to print my name. I looked forward to the day when I could go to school like Wally on *Leave It to Beaver*. Wally was always doing homework and making school look like fun.

Finally the big day came in 1958—I was six and ready to start school. I was excited as Mom and I went to school orientation the day before school officially started. At first we all met together, mothers and children, until it was time for the mothers to leave for their own meeting. When Mom got up to leave, I followed her right out the door and cried in the hallway. They couldn't make me go back in the room with the other first graders.

Mom was a little embarrassed, but the principal came by and bent down to talk to me.

"Hi. What's your name? Cindy? Well, Cindy, you need to let your mother go in with the other mothers, and you can go in with the other first-grade children. I'm sure you will be fine."

He was very nice and comforting, but I would not be persuaded. I went in with mom and the other adults. Oddly enough, when the first real day of school came, I was fine.

Akron Elementary was a one-story, yellow block building across from the older red-brick high school. There was no kindergarten, so a child would start in first grade at one end of the long hall and advance from room to room, year by year, down the hallway, then make a left turn into the new section to reach fifth grade.

My first-grade teacher was Mrs. Kinder, like *kinder*, the German word for children. Mrs. Kinder stood straight and tall, a dignified woman who had taught school for many years. She could be kind and patient while teaching children to read, but she could also be stern and forceful, not afraid to shake little boys by the shoulders to make them behave. I never got in trouble because I was the teacher's pet. I listened quietly and did everything that was expected of me. I sat with my reading group, identified by color, in a circle of little chairs with Mrs. Kinder, reading stories about Dick and Jane, Sally, Spot the dog, and Puff the cat.

As early as first grade, I was attracted to the boys, but one boy caused me to live in fear for a while. His name was Ronnie. He was a husky bully with curly red hair and freckles. I don't remember how he teased me or scared me, but I was afraid to go to school and tried to keep older stronger people around me. One day at recess, I hid in the bushes because of Ronnie. I was still there after everyone had gone inside, so Mrs. Kinder had to send someone out to find me. But I eventually got over it and moved on to second grade.

Year by year, I moved down that elementary hall, making valentines, silhouettes of Lincoln and Washington, hand-print turkeys, and a diorama of Switzerland. I brought home report cards full of As. We took field trips to the Milnot factory in Warsaw and the Seyferts potato-chip factory in Fort Wayne.

Mindy and I were always one of the very first ones on the school bus. It was only five miles to Akron, but it took forty-five minutes to get there, zig-zagging from house to house through the countryside to fill up the bus. On chilly winter mornings, we were up before sunrise, sitting half-awake on the wooden bench Daddy had built over the kitchen radiator, limply holding out arms and legs for Mom to dress us. We girls wore dresses to school all the time, even in the winter. We just put on tights, little red boots, hats, and mittens. Then we added snow pants if it was really cold.

Mom fixed us breakfast and made sure we had everything we needed while the WOWO radio station perked in the background and the deep voice of Bob Sievers brought us the news. We passed through the store to the front door, then watched for the bus through the little panes of glass covered with Jack Frost designs. During the long bus ride, I daydreamed day after day while look-ing out the window, listening to the familiar hiss of the bus brakes and the jangle of the radio.

The bus ride was boring except for one exciting trip home when the bus couldn't make it up a slippery hill in a snowstorm. As we tried to go forward, the bus slipped backwards toward the opposite side of the road and a steep ravine. We were on a lonely country road about a mile north of Disko.

The bus driver had no choice but to say, "Get out, kids. We're walking to Disko." The snow fell around my cold feet and legs, but we walked that mile home to Disko.

I agreed with Andy Williams about Christmas: "It's the most wonderful time of the year." I loved the long, dark evenings, the Christmas tree in the living room, the sparkly snow falling, and the anticipation of something wonderful about to happen. We didn't believe in Santa Claus because we knew who bought the presents and we knew it was Jesus' birth we were celebrating. We couldn't miss the nativity scene clustered on the Rochester courthouse lawn with its giant camels and larger-than-life figures of shepherds and wise men around the Baby Jesus in the manger. Back then, nobody was offended by a nativity scene displayed on government property.

We bought a real evergreen tree each year, just a week or two before Christmas, then decorated it with strings of big colored light bulbs, assorted ornaments, and strands of silver icicles. We did this together with Mom, bringing the tattered cardboard boxes of Christmas stuff out of the storage room. As soon as Mom bought presents, she wrapped them and placed them under the tree so we could shake the boxes and try to guess what was inside.

Because we didn't have to wait for Santa to come during the night, Christmas Eve was our special time. After supper, when it was dark and silent like the original Christmas night, or so we imagined, with snow on the ground and Christmas lights all around, it was the perfect time for the opening of the gifts. We distributed each colorful package from under the tree, and then everyone opened their gifts at once. Mindy and I ripped off the wrapping paper in a frenzy. It was all over in just a few minutes, but Mindy and I were never disappointed. We always had lots of gifts—toys, games, cowboy outfits, coloring books, and clothes. We had a little time to play and admire our new things while Mom cleaned up the boxes and paper, but then it was time for bed.

On Christmas Day, we went to Grandma and Grandpa Gearhart's house in Akron. Daddy always dressed up that day, putting on a nice shirt and pants, then his heavy tweed overcoat. I think he only wore that coat one time a year. Daddy drove us into Akron as a family, which was a special event in itself because Mom always took us everywhere else. Daddy didn't travel anywhere except to Gearhart family functions.

My dad's parents were Frank and Edna Gearhart. Frank was German; his grandfather George was actually born in Germany. The Gearharts came to America and passed through Pennsylvania until they got to Indiana, and then they stopped. Frank's family never really left the area after that. They all lived within fifty miles of Akron; if they ever did move any farther away, they all eventually moved back.

I asked Mom and Daddy, "Am I German or Irish? With all the McPeaks, McQuistons, and McWilliams, shouldn't I be three-fourths Irish?"

Daddy said emphatically, "No, you're mostly German"—because that's what he wanted us to be.

He was proud to say that he was German. When he was in Germany, he loved their land and the way they lived. "You never saw any trash in the streets or any junk cars sitting in their yards," he said.

Frank Gearhart was a thin, wiry man with cool blue-gray eyes and a chin held high in pride and determination. Edna McPeak was Irish, round in face and body, with brown, friendly eyes. She provided love and warmth for their sixteen children, and Frank provided the discipline. They both labored, raising eleven boys and five girls through the Depression, WWII, and the Korean War. Seven of their sons served in the armed forces, stationed at different times in Panama, Greenland, Europe, Korea, and the South Pacific. Frank worked as a foreman for the Erie Lackawanna Railroad as they built new tracks in northern Indiana. The Erie Lackawanna connected the towns of Huntington, Laketon, Disko, Akron, Athens, and Rochester, and then went all the way to Chicago. It was hard work, but it was a steady job through the Depression. Frank even managed to save a little money, thinking it would support him in his old age, but never realizing how times would change.

There were actually eighteen children born to the Gearharts, but one set of twins died of pneumonia a few months after their birth. Mom said Grandma grieved for years over the loss of the twins, even though she had so many other children. My dad was born after Ray, Opal, Floyd, Leonard, and the twins. After him came Harold, Leo, Dorothy, Bill, Max, Ruth, Dick, Sharon, Larry, Joan, and Roger—in that order.

I asked Mom how they managed to take care of so many kids. She said, "Everyone just worked harder in those days and didn't think anything about it. They didn't have any modern conveniences. But sometimes Grandma would get discouraged and go off into another room and cry, so the kids couldn't see her; then she'd come back and keep going on."

Even though the Gearharts were better off than many, it was still a struggle. They sometimes went to school without shoes, or they would only have one pair. Several kids would sleep in the same bed. But they all grew up with the will to work hard and make a place for themselves in the world. Many of the boys became businessmen, and some were very successful. Harold, Bill, Max, Dick, Roger, and Larry were all involved at one time or another in the grocery business, like Daddy and Leo.

Uncle Leo was absent from my Gearhart Christmases. He had fought in World War II and the Korean War, and then he joined my dad in running The Old Dutch Mill. He was married and had a son. One day he was helping to put a TV antenna on a house in Disko. Leo tried to hold the tall antenna steady, but it fell onto an electric line, electrocuting him and causing him to fall from the roof. It was a horrifying day for the family, most especially for my dad. Leo had been the family favorite, good-looking and loved by everyone. After he died, some of my dad's hair even fell out from the grief. Mom said that was why he always had a little bald patch on the back on his head. But life went on without Leo, and I only knew him as a mischievous smiling face in the Gearhart family photo.

Because the Gearhart family was so large, there was always a rollicking crowd when we went to Grandma and Grandpa's for Christmas. Everyone in the family came, including a troop of cousins, several of whom were my age. Grandma and Grandpa would sit in easy chairs, as if resting after so many years of work, with all their children and grandchildren milling around them. Some of my aunts and uncles were very quiet and withdrawn like my dad, but others were talkative and social. One or two were even involved in politics. The women were petite, some weighing barely one hundred pounds, and the men were of average build, none over six feet tall. Most people in the family had bushy eyebrows and thin lips.

The Gearharts enjoyed being together. While I played with the cousins, the uncles always had a card game going on in the living room with much laughing and teasing and arguing. The Gearharts talked fast. Words came out in a rapid string and ended in a nervous laugh.

The women worked in the kitchen getting all the good food ready. Grandma Gearhart made homemade noodles, cut as thin as spaghetti so it tasted better. All my aunts ever did was work, it seemed to me. As soon as we were finished eating, they spent the rest of the day cleaning up, standing over the sink washing dishes. But they didn't complain. They talked together while they worked and had a good time.

In the front living room was a big Christmas tree with presents spilling out to cover most of the floor. Late in the afternoon, Uncle Roger knocked at the front door, dressed like Santa Claus. He came in jolly and laughing to pass out the gifts, usually a sweater for each of us kids from Grandma, until buying gifts became too big of a job for her and then we exchanged names. Sometimes there would be gag gifts from one brother to another because they liked to play practical jokes on each other.

Grandma and Grandpa Gearhart both lived long lives. Grandma Gearhart died when she was seventy-one and was buried on the Fourth of July in 1968. Grandpa Gearhart lived to be one hundred and two and died in 1987. Mom said one reason Grandpa lived so long was because he lived such a regular life, always getting up, going to bed, and eating at the same time each day. He mowed his own yard by hand until he was in his nineties and walked downtown each day to sit and talk with the other old men of Akron.

Our family doctor was Dr. Herrick, who had a little office just off Main Street in Akron. Dr. Herrick had been there for my birth at Woodlawn Hospital in Rochester, Indiana. I still have the bill for that three-day hospital stay, which totaled $45.47. The hospital room cost $7 a day, the delivery room was $15, drugs were $3.47, and the nursery was $6.

Mindy and I were taken to Dr. Herrick for our smallpox vaccinations and polio shots—and any other time when we had a sore throat or other childhood ailment that required penicillin. After sitting in the little waiting room, we were taken to the treatment room that looked much like a Norman Rockwell painting. I gazed at the doctor's desk, the tall canister with tongue depressors, the bottles of pills, and the unknown gadgets. It smelled like medicine and alcohol. Dr. Herrick was a middle-aged man, but he was unmarried and lived with his mother.

We didn't have to see the doctor very often because most of our health care was given at home. Mom became our nurse when we were sick. She took our temperature and gave us liquids if we had a fever. If it was a stomach problem, we got Pepto-Bismol or Rolaids, and Mom set up two chairs together in the bathroom like a bed so we could sleep near the toilet. When we had the measles, we were kept in the dark to protect our eyes. If I was at school feeling chills and fatigue, sure signs that a cold or flu was coming on, there was no better feeling than finally getting home to be cared for by Mom and knowing I wouldn't have to go to school the next day.

I never had a serious injury because of Mom's warnings, "Don't run with scissors or knives. You might fall and stab yourself."

"Don't run with a sucker in your mouth, or you might jam it down your throat."

Daddy said, "Get down from there, or you'll fall and crack your head open." I always thought a fractured skull would be like a cracked-open melon.

The only injury I really can remember clearly was a burn on my hand. I reached into a pile of burning trash to pick up a metal pipe I felt like I needed. Of course, it was blazing hot, and I blistered my palm. I ran all around our big sports field, shaking my hand and yelling. When Mom and Daddy caught up with me, they put Vaseline on my hand and wrapped it up. I only mention it because it's the only injury I ever had.

Our dentist was Dr. Sparks, whose office was on Main Street in Rochester. The door to his second-story office was wedged between two storefronts and read, "Dr. Sparks D.D.S." on its glass window. We climbed the worn wooden stairs upward into semi-darkness to reach his office. It was a somber trip, not only because of the dingy stairway, but because we were about to get fillings put in our teeth. In the waiting room, I looked at *Highlight* magazines, reading the stories, finding the missing objects in the pictures, and doing the puzzles, trying to keep my mind off the reason we were there. We went to the dentist quite often because we needed fillings in most of our molars—maybe because of all the Hershey bars and Fudgesickles from the store.

Dr. Sparks seemed very old to me. He was tall and thin, with a lined, whiskery face. He leaned over and talked to us while he worked on our teeth, getting his smoky breath on our faces. Mom chatted with him during our appointment and afterwards when we paid the bill, which was only a few dollars for each filling. He didn't seem to be in a hurry. If Mindy and I had been good, he gave us each a dime.

Once we got in a discussion about God, and he tried to make us question our childlike faith. He was a learned, worldly man, and Mom said he shouldn't cause little children to stumble concerning their faith. He said we needed to learn to think for ourselves.

He once asked me, "Did you know that your dad is an existentialist? Do you know what an existentialist is?"

I said, "No."

He said, "It means your dad makes his own decisions and lives as a unique individual."

One day as we stood at the top of the stairs to leave, I said to Dr. Sparks, "Did you know it says 'skraps' when you look at your name on the door from up here?"

He said, "I've gone up and down these stairs for forty years and never saw that before!"

Akron had two funeral homes for use when people died. One was Sheetz Funeral Home, and the other was Harris Funeral Home. We always chose Sheetz when we needed to bury someone, because Mr. Sheetz looked and acted the most like a funeral director. He had a long, sad face covered in deep creases, almost like it had been mummified. He seemed to represent death better than Mr. Harris did. We felt like he sympathized with us and cared about the person who had died. Mr. Harris was younger and just too happy. I think that was why he never got our business.

CHAPTER 3

Lord, through all the generations, You have been our home!

PSALM 90:1

Mom attended the Disko Methodist church, a simple white-frame building with a steeple and church bell. Shortly after I was born, she saw her need for God's help in her life and became a Christian. Mom took an active part in the church, taking us with her to all the services. Although we could see the church from the gas pumps of The Dutch Mill, we were always a few minutes late. At different times over the years, Mom was the church treasurer, a Sunday school teacher, and the president of WSCS, the Women's Society for Christian Service. She attended weekly Bible-study meetings and brought food to all the church functions, usually baked beans with crispy bacon on top.

The little church could hold two hundred people, but our average attendance and offering each Sunday was about forty people and forty dollars . Amber-stained glass windows lined the sanctuary, and rows of wooden pews stood on either side of a center aisle. Behind the pulpit was a picture of Jesus in the Garden of Gethsemane, and to the right was the upright piano that accompanied our singing from the Methodist hymnal. The basement rooms were used for potluck dinners and kids' Sunday school classrooms, while the adults had Sunday school upstairs, young adults in one corner and older adults in the other. Mom usually taught one of these adult classes.

On each Mother's Day, flowers were given to the mother with the most children, the oldest mother, and the youngest mother who had attended church that day. Grandma didn't go to church every Sunday morning, but she was always present for Mother's Day, hoping to win the prize for oldest mother—and she usually did.

Grandma loved to ask people with a smile, "Now, how old do you think I am?" She liked to outsmart them, because she thought she looked much younger than she actually was.

Mom was not only a member of the WSCS, but she also belonged to the Fulton County Homemakers' Club, a gathering of about a dozen women from the local area. Both of these groups met once a month in the homes of the various women. Mindy and I went along to play with the other kids. I have no idea what the women did at these meetings, but they always ended with refreshments. The most popular desert was Jello, green or orange, with cottage cheese, served on glass plates shaped like a leaf with a little spot outlined for your cup.

I learned to cook by watching Mom. She taught me how to make Daddy's favorite cake, German chocolate, when I was no more than twelve years old. Mindy and I liked to be around the kitchen when Mom made desserts, asking to lick out the bowl and reaching in for a taste of batter. If all the ingredients hadn't been added yet, she would get frustrated, saying, "Don't eat that! It's just butter and sugar. You're going to throw off the proportions!"

Over the years she taught us how to fry chicken, make gravy, whip up mashed potatoes, cook roast beef with vegetables, prepare Jello, and mix milkshakes. She gave us some old recipe books, and we practiced cooking outside, using different kinds of dirt and plants for the ingredients.

Mom didn't like to use packaged mixes, but we did try the Kraft pizza mix. We had never eaten pizza before and wanted to see what it was like. Inside the box were the crust ingredients, a can of pizza sauce, and parmesan cheese. That was all. After we baked and tasted it, we wondered why people thought pizza was so special. Daddy said, "You don't need to make pizza again."

Mom didn't need box mixes. She made nourishing meals, always with a variety of dishes and always including fruits and vegetables. She made homemade soups and breads, and she always served cottage cheese. There were always cookies and desserts, too.

I learned how to clean house by watching Mom. I learned that the best time to clean house is right before company comes! Mom kept the kitchen and other important areas clean all the time, of course, but when she was going to host a meeting with the ladies, she got serious and cleaned and dusted everywhere. Then she washed the curtains and the windows and took down all the knick-knacks, like the green elephant and the rooster family, and washed them off.

Mom's theory was that a house was meant to be lived in. She said, "It's more important to be comfortable and allow your kids to be creative than to have a perfect house that's so sterile and proper a person can't enjoy it."

Mom encouraged creativity in our house. We had stacks of coloring books, boxes of crayons, watercolors, scissors, and puzzles to use at any time. We kept all this creative stuff in the kitchen in a homemade cupboard, built out of knotty pine, of course. At times it would get so full and messy that we would decide to clean it out. After we pulled everything out onto the kitchen floor, Mindy and I would look things over and start to reorganize, but we would soon tire of the job and leave the rest to Mom. She also let us build tents in the living room by stretching blankets across chairs and pinning them down with books.

She did her best to keep the house presentable and clean with two little girls and the store to tend. I just thought it couldn't be helped that bedrooms were dusty, countertops were cluttered, and the space behind the toilet was a dank, spidery place.

We knew all the families that lived in Disko (population two hundred), including a family I'll call the Allens. Their names, and others in this book, have been changed for the sake of privacy. Next to Frank Peters' grocery store and post office, the Allens lived in an old, clapboard store building that faced Main Street and extended far back behind. I never actually went inside their home, but I imagined a big open area with a high ceiling, a kitchen at one end, beds at the other end, and junk lying all around. They were poor and seemed a little mysterious to me.

One of the older girls in their family would occasionally come into The Dutch Mill. I noticed that her stomach kept getting bigger, although her arms and legs were thin. I thought she had cancer or some other disease, but it turned out she was just having a baby, even though she wasn't married. I wondered how God knew who was married and who should get the babies.

Jimmy Allen was Mike's age. He hung around the store, pushing me up and down the aisles on my tricycle. He was a good friend of Mike's, and he sometimes helped my dad. He came to the store and ate candy bars and drank Coke. Mom said, "I think that's all Jimmy Allen ever eats."

But Jimmy was always nice to me. Once when Mike and Jimmy were playing Monopoly, Jimmy let me be the banker, handing out deeds and money, even though I wasn't old enough to read yet.

Mike said, "You can't play with us. Go dry up."

I wanted to be with the boys because I thought the boys had more fun. Mike, Jimmy, and their friends would sit at the counter in the store, dropping peanuts in their cokes and then drinking them, so I would do the same. Jimmy had long, curly dark hair. I watched the way he combed his hair, then I looked in the mirror and combed mine the same way. I wanted to play sports with the neighborhood boys, but I just didn't fit in because I was a girl. I didn't value my uniqueness as a girl at the time. I thought the boys would like me if I was just one of them.

As we grew older, Mindy and I were free to roam around Disko and play with the girls our age. We went to their houses, and they came to ours. We all dressed up as cowboys, or we splashed around in little wading pools in only our shorts. We thought nothing of walking around town with naked torsos even at the age of nine or ten.

Summertime was long in those days in Disko. When we came inside the house on a summer day, we heard the comforting sound of a baseball game on the big, brown radio that sat on the floor in the hallway. Daddy liked the Chicago White Sox. Regardless of what was going on in the world, it seemed that all was well if you could hear the sound of a baseball game in the background.

On hot summer evenings, we stayed out late, playing in the yard, catching lightning bugs that winked all around us, and putting them in a jar for a nightlight. I often heard mourning doves in the evening, which would make me feel melancholy. Mom would call us inside and we'd take a bath, and then she would wave us dry with a bath towel like an Indian sending smoke signals. We went to sleep with the glass windchimes tinkling outside the bedroom window.

When storms blew in on summer afternoons, we watched the rain come in from the southwest like a silvery sheet moving right across the field, pattering down on the plants, until it reached us in a downpour. We smelled the wet earth even before it got to us. Sometimes the storms blew in with a vengeance, and we watched our elm trees bend over and toss around. On humid stormy nights, we watched "heat lightning," as we called it, flashing in all directions on the horizon.

One summer day we went to Zeno Schultz's farm just south of Akron to pick out a pony. What little girl doesn't want a pony? Zeno and his wife had that hardy "outdoors, blue-jeans" look that people have who own horses. Zeno showed us his ponies, and we chose a dappled tan one, with a lighter mane and tail. We named him Dandy. His nose really did feel as soft as velvet. We kept Dandy for a while, and later we even got a darker pony named Dusty, but we didn't keep them long because, as we discovered, ponies are a whole lot of trouble.

After several years of storekeeping, my mom and dad decided to close The Old Dutch Mill in the late 1950s. My dad was starting to get carpentry and remodeling jobs, and he wanted to get out of the grocery business. They first closed the food counter, then the garage, and then decided that it was time for the whole store to close.

I asked Daddy if they had made a lot of money with the store, and he replied, "The Dutch Mill never made any money."

I wasn't sure what he meant by that. We always had everything we really wanted. As a child living behind that store, I had never been aware of the adult responsibilities going on around me. Someone had ordered the products for the store, stocked the shelves, paid the bills, and made the decisions, while every day I had played in the back yard or watched TV. I didn't have to carry the heavy suitcase of adult worries and issues—my parents carried it for me.

Daddy was a dreamer, and his plans kept growing. He bought the old clubhouse in Disko, remodeled it, and then sold it as a house. Next he bought the Schultz house and began working on it. He could picture how a house could be remodeled or built, and then just do it. Finally came his greatest vision of all, to buy an eighty-acre patch of land about a mile from Disko. He bought it for nine thousand dollars. It wasn't much good for farming because it was hilly and had swampy areas, but it had a beautiful woods and a creek flowing through it. A barn stood by the highway with "Chew Mail Pouch Tobacco" painted on one side.

Daddy loved that farm. He parked our car along the gravel road where the creek passed underneath, and made us tramp through fields of waist-high grass up the hill to the woods. He usually had to carry Mindy, but I was able to keep up. From the top of the hill we could see across a broad valley as far as the hills north of Disko. We had picnics there by a flat rock, and he shared his dream with us of one day building a house right in that spot. We thought it was an impossible dream.

After our picnic, we walked through more high grass and bushes down to the creek. Mindy and I loved to play in the creek in the shallow area where we could wade across. I looked through the clear water at the smooth rocks and watched crawdads dart around. Sometimes I found mussel shells or saw a snake's head above the water. We also had picnics there by the creek, and Daddy built a bridge across it.

In the summer we planted a garden at the foot of the hill by a giant sycamore tree where the ground was moist and springy. It wasn't convenient, being a mile from our home and far back from the road, but it was on our new land. We helped Mom and Daddy plant the garden and then hoe it. In July we picked black raspberries from thickets of raspberry bushes in the woods. We had to wear long sleeves and pants, even though it was hot, in order to protect our arms and legs from scratches and mosquitoes. We picked gallons of raspberries that Mom smashed and strained through cheesecloth to make jelly, which was then poured into little jars and covered with paraffin. In the fall, we helped harvest the garden, and Mom canned green beans and tomatoes and made pickles.

Daddy tried his hand at raising pigs and calves on his farm, putting the calves in the barn and the pigs in the shed. Mindy and I were eager to go with him in the evenings to feed the animals. The pigs ate buttermilk that was kept in a big barrel. As we walked into the barn, there was always a sour smell as Daddy scooped out feed for the calves and put down new straw for them. When it was time for the sows to have babies, we went with Daddy at night and looked over the fence to see birth happen.

On my ninth birthday, I received a five-year diary. Being a studious little girl, I wrote faithfully in my diary for the next five years, recording each day's events in a space about the size of a wide Band-Aid. I recorded the weather and the highlights of the day in my own shorthand phrases, keeping track of who we visited, how many baby pigs were born, or how many cookies we made that day.

As I grew older, I became a little scientist. I collected fossils, bones, and locust shells that I lined up on a shelf in the old store. I liked to read about dinosaurs. When I got a microscope for Christmas, I examined pond water for invisible creatures and studied things from around the house, like onion peels and cockroach legs. (Yes, the cockroaches were from our own house. Mom said it was because we lived behind a grocery store, and it couldn't be helped because they came in with the boxes of produce. She tried different remedies but couldn't get rid of them. I thought everybody's house had cockroaches. They hid during the day, but if I turned on the kitchen light at night, I could watch them scurry away.) I thought I would like to be an archaeologist or a scientist of some kind when I grew up.

Mom took Mindy and me wherever we needed to go, whether shopping or on errands or to the dentist. She always seemed to be in a hurry, trotting across the street to a store, then back again to the car. She trotted any short distance, for no reason, as if someone was waiting for her to hurry up. If we were in town long enough, she took us to a restaurant for lunch, especially after trips to the dentist. She took us to all of our school functions. When I was in the fourth grade, she attended the school festival to watch me do the hula dance in a crepe-paper grass skirt. She also took me to the school Halloween contest—I was dressed as an Indian, in a loincloth, with a homemade hatchet, and wearing flesh-colored tights that made me look like I was naked. I won a silver dollar for third prize.

Sometimes Mom took alternate routes to get somewhere just so we could see different parts of the countryside and other places of interest. She loved the autumn leaves, and she liked to point out the round barns and covered bridges.

If Grandma was with us on a drive, she always contributed a running commentary on other people's yards. "Look at the pretty flowers! Oh, my goodness! And that house right beside it doesn't have anything. I don't understand why some people don't have any flowers," Grandma would say.

Listening to her quaint way of talking one day, Mindy and I decided to imitate her.

"Goodness gracious sakes alive!" I said.

"My land. My goodness! For heaven's sakes! For crying out loud," Mindy replied.

Mom had heard enough. She said, "Don't mock Grandma!"

I hadn't thought of it as mocking, but we learned a lesson. We never did it again.

As we grew older, Mindy and I observed our mom and dad more closely. We noted that while Mom was very casual at home, she always wanted to look nice in public. She never left the house without putting on her lipstick. Mindy and I noticed she even talked differently in public with people she considered important. She wanted her speech to sound correct, and her voice actually changed. She had her own very real sense of dignity. When she dressed up, she always wore earrings to match her dress, and she had a variety of pins and necklaces to go with different outfits. The Avon representative who came to our house was always able to sell Mom something until our entire bathroom counter was cluttered with scented creams, perfume, and lipstick. The bathroom smelled like powdery flowers.

Mom was frustrated that she gained weight as she grew older, but Daddy liked to joke about how broad she was. In order to look her best when she had her picture taken, she always put one leg a little in front of the other to make her hips look smaller, and she always smiled a prim and proper smile.

Daddy never had a weight problem. He gained a few pounds in the winter and lost those same pounds in the summer. He ate until he'd had enough and then he just stopped, even if it meant leaving one bite of food on his plate, which he often did. Mom packed him a variety of things in his lunch bucket, but he usually brought one thing back uneaten. Mom, Mindy, and I couldn't understand someone who didn't want to overeat. Because he worked hard all day, eating lightly, he was able to eat a whole handful of cookies while watching TV in the evening, or make a sandwich or a milkshake during the commercials. The rest of us ate along with him, and we all gained weight.

Daddy never went to any public events or school functions, but we never held it against him. We were content with his presence at home, and even though he didn't say, "I love you" every day, we knew he adored his girls. Daddy's way of spending time with us was just by being there every evening, a dependable rock we could always count on. He was very uncomfortable in social situations and avoided them whenever possible, unlike Mom, who would go out of her way in town or in the grocery store to speak to someone she knew, or even to someone she didn't know. Daddy only took us to places related to his family or to his work, such as to houses he was working on or Miller and Sons Lumber Company.

Daddy did take me mushroom hunting, though. We took our paper sacks and looked in the woods along the railroad tracks for yellow sponge or leggy spikes. We never found very many, but I developed a love for the search. On one trip, when I was still short enough that my paper sack drug against the wet grass, we got home only to find that all of our mushrooms had fallen out the bottom of the soggy sack.

CHAPTER 4

Many families take a vacation every year, but our family took only one vacation—ever. I was nine years old when we went with Elaine and her husband, Harold, to his family home in Paintsburg, Kentucky.

Harold was Elaine's second husband. She had married Doyle Heckaman shortly after graduating from high school, and they lived in a trailer at Diamond Lake, where their son, Jaime, was born on Mindy's second birthday. Doyle was mild mannered and industrious, but their marriage didn't work out. Elaine then married Harold Ousley, a good-looking man from Kentucky. The Ousleys were one of a group of families who had moved to Indiana from Paintsburg, Kentucky, to get better jobs. They settled in Packerton, where some of them lived in little shack-like houses very different from what we were used to. Harold was likable and worked hard but he had a drinking problem, as well as an anger problem. They lived in Kokomo, Indiana, for several years where Harold managed a filling station, and their first daughter, Sheryl Yvonne, was born there. Elaine almost died from complications after her childbirth.

Harold and Elaine decided to take us to Kentucky. After staying the night in Kokomo and dropping Grandma off with Aunt Inez, we all piled into the car—Mom, Daddy, Mindy, me, Elaine, Harold, and Sheryl Yvonne. It was a hot July day, our bare legs stuck to the seats, but we were on our first vacation. We drove south, and I watched with wonder as we saw little hills in southern Indiana and then finally came to the Ohio River. I had never been this far from home. I looked out the window at the broad river and the jumble of tall buildings, which was Louisville, on the other side.

Mom said, "When we cross the river, we will be in Kentucky."

Farther south we began to move between larger hills. After stopping to eat a picnic lunch at a roadside table, we finally started twisting between the mountains of eastern Kentucky and eventually arrived at Paintsville. We turned onto a smaller road leading more deeply into the mountains, and seemingly more deeply into the past. The valley was narrow. Elaine said that some people were born in these "hollers," and lived and died there, without ever leaving. Planted against the hillside, I spotted an occasional wooden house with haphazard outbuildings and dogs or chickens scattered about. A few miles down the road, we reached the Ousley family home. It was a house like the others, with a front porch up on stilts, a barn, and a hill rising straight up in back.

We got out of the car and were greeted by the family. Harold asked where his brother was, and they said, "He's down at the born."

I realized he meant the barn. Right away I loved their Kentucky accent.

"Y'all come inside now," they said.

Harold's mom seemed glad to meet us and made us feel at home. We went through the screen door into their homey, clean house, and she showed us our bedroom. The next morning, she made us a breakfast of homemade biscuits and gravy with sausage and eggs. They had electricity, but they pulled their water out of a well in a bucket and had an outhouse for their bathroom. I felt like I was in another world and another time. It rained the next day, so I learned how to play Rook with Harold's eleven-year-old twin brother and sister. We sat on the porch for hours while it rained a steamy rain.

After we left the Ousley's, we spent the next three days sightseeing in Kentucky. We went to Cumberland Falls, Mammoth Cave, and Lincoln's birthplace. Each day we ate at a roadside table or a restaurant for lunch, and each evening we chose a motel for the night, with a name like "Shady Side Inn" or "Starlite Motel."

It was all an adventure to us, traveling with our family, eating and sleeping away from home. Daddy bought us souvenirs, a little painted Indian bowl for me and a bank for Mindy. We drove back to Indiana, picked up Grandma in Kokomo, and then went home. I'll never forget our one and only family vacation.

But Elaine's life with Harold was not easy. They had fights, and she had to move back home temporarily while Harold spent some time in jail for drunk driving. After they had a second daughter, Cherileen, they moved into Grandma's house in Disko, and Grandma moved in with us. Harold started working at the Dalton Foundry in Warsaw, and it seemed that surely things were getting better. They had a son, Richie, while living in Disko.

I visited them sometimes, and I liked Harold with his easy smile. Watching Elaine fix biscuits and fried chicken, I thought it would be fun to be married and cook for a husband. I liked the country music always playing at their house, with singers like Johnny Cash and Marty Robbins and albums like *Johnny Rivers Live at the Whisky-a-go-go*. One summer, Harold built a fence around their property, and I helped him paint it white. It was fun to work with Harold doing a grown-up job like painting. I hoped everything was going to be better for Elaine and Harold, but I knew that he had an ulcer and that he sometimes threw up after he ate dinner.

Several years later, we were watching TV one evening when we decided to have some ice cream with homemade chocolate topping. I was stirring the chocolate sauce on the stove when someone pounded on the front door. We answered the door to find a neighbor from Disko shouting, "Harold killed hisself!"

Harold had shot himself with a rifle and was lying dead in his kitchen.

Harold and Elaine had still been having problems, but I just hadn't known it because the adults had protected me from it and I never saw Harold drunk or angry. After he got home from work that day, he had taken out his rifle, threatening to do something violent. Elaine took the kids and ran outside—and then she heard the shot.

We took care of their little kids that night and gave them baths, and the adults did what they could to help Elaine. It was a horrible time.

I didn't understand why anyone would kill himself. Mom said a teenager had killed himself in the round upstairs tower in a house in Akron. Whenever we drove by that house, I'd look at that tower and think about the boy killing himself there. And why did George Reeves, the actor who played Superman, kill himself? It was hard to understand. It was a sad story with a sad ending for Harold. It was one of the first funerals I ever went to.

It wasn't the end of the story for Elaine, though. She was left to care for her two little girls and little Richie, who looked just like his dad. After living in the same house for some time, she met a man who would help her forget the past—Riley Shepherd. He looked like a cowboy from an old western, tall and lean in jeans and cowboy boots. He spoke in a low monotone, much like John Wayne, and smoked all the time. He was divorced with four kids about the same ages as Elaine's girls.

They got married and lived in Silver Lake. Elaine told us stories of how she managed with those seven kids. I was amazed. She had to organize everything from coats and shoes to daily schedules. She learned to buy and cook in large quantities. She faced rivalry and jealousy among the kids as she tried to blend them into one family. I admired her that she could do something like that. Elaine and Riley eventually moved to South Dakota, near Mount Rushmore, and had a child of their own, Clint. Elaine went back to school and became a successful realtor.

My brother, Mike, loved fishing and sports of all kinds, especially basketball. He was one of the starting five players for the Akron Flyers, pictured in the yearbook throwing a hook shot over his shoulder. Mom, Mindy, and I went to the basketball games, but even though Mike was a good player, the Flyers usually lost their games. Sometimes they led in all the quarters but the last one, as I recorded in my diary. Mike was the "basketball king" during his senior year. He also had a girlfriend that year.

Mindy and I liked Mike's girlfriend, Judy Hutchinson, because she had a horse and she would play with us when she came to see Mike. We loved to visit her home in hopes of riding the horse. She did spend time with Mike, and they soon grew serious enough that they got married after Mike graduated from high school. Mike went to Manchester College for one year, and then became an apprentice at R.R. Donnelley's, a company that published catalogs. Mom said that one year in college had made Mike more polished. Mike and Judy had a son named Aaron, but their marriage didn't work out, and they got a divorce.

I was still in elementary school when Mike graduated. Each week at school, our class would walk several blocks downtown through leaves or snow to the Akron Library to check out books. I liked horse stories, Hardy Boy mysteries, and science-fiction space stories about rockets flying to the moon or to other planets. Usually there were aliens on those planets. I listened to the news about the United States sending the first men into space and racing with Russia to get a man onto the moon, so it wasn't just science fiction anymore. I thought it was fascinating.

I studied Mike's *Little Golden Book of Stars* and then tried to locate the constellations outside. The illustrations in the book showed the stars connected like dot-to-dot puzzles to form mythological figures in the sky. I watched the hunter Orion rise on a cold winter night next to the brightest star, Sirius. The frosty nights made the stars twinkle even brighter. On hot, hazy summer nights, I saw Scorpius like a real scorpion lying just above the southern horizon and the glittery stream of the Milky Way overhead. I ordered a ten-cent telescope through the mail from *Encyclopedia Britannica*. It was about a foot long and set on a little tripod. After impatiently waiting until dark, I watched the stars come out, one by one. I picked out the patterns of the constellations, focused on a double star or a planet, and then drug Mom outside so she could enjoy it with me.

My favorite science-fiction movie was *Invaders from Mars*. A little boy watches from his bedroom as a flying saucer lands in the field behind his house. People start acting strangely, including his parents, and eventually he ends up in the underground tunnels made by the aliens. The goon-like aliens with long arms run along the tunnels, which have shiny, pebbly walls, and he discovers that the aliens are implanting a device in the back of people's heads to control them. In the end, the boy wakes up, and it was all a dream, but then as he looks out the bedroom window, he sees the flying saucer rising from the ground. So you just never knew.

I also watched *Shock Theater* on TV late at night. I saw *Frankenstein*, *Dracula*, the werewolf, the invisible man, and the mummy. I liked to be scared, and I ignored the warnings that these shows were "not suitable for impressionable children." *The Twilight Zone* was another favorite of mine. One episode showed a little girl falling from her bed through the wall into the fourth dimension, and then she had trouble getting back. I could always scare Mindy by saying she was going to fall into the fourth dimension.

My fifth-grade classroom was in the new wing at Akron Elementary. The fresh, new cork floors and new books had a wonderful smell. I had my first male teacher, a tall skinny man named Mr. Becraft. I began to single out boys who I liked, such as Byron Tinkey, who was easy to flirt with because he sat behind me in class. To show our elementary-school affection, we would trip each other in the hallways.

At recess, we girls played tag or jump rope because the boys usually had control of the basketball courts. We sang little jingles as we jumped rope, counting until we missed a step to see how many babies we were going to have when we grew up. When the school got a tether-ball, that became my favorite sport. I loved the feel of my fist hitting the ball and swinging it over the other person's head.

I wasn't chosen to be a cheerleader in fifth grade, but I did win the school spelling bee. I qualified to go to the next level, which was going to be on the radio. I studied the book of possible words to get ready for my first time on the air. All of the contestants sat in a circle in a glassed-in sound room at the Warsaw radio station. We started the first round, and I was third in line. My word was *account*. I said a-c-o-u-n-t, and just like that, I was out. I was the first person down, on my first word—and on the radio. It was embarrassing and disappointing. I made up for it in sixth grade by winning the school spelling bee again and coming in third at the regional contest.

My fifth-grade science project was an egg incubator, a cardboard box with a glowing lightbulb inside. My idea was to get some eggs to actually hatch. I would open a few along the way and display them in glass jars to show the stages of the baby chick's growth, like I had seen in the encyclopedia.

Mom said, "You'll need to get fertilized eggs from a farmer to make it work."

I wasn't sure what she meant, because I only had a hazy idea about reproduction in either people or chickens, but I said, "Okay. Fine with me."

So, that's what we did. But it didn't work. I faithfully tended the incubator, as it glowed with a warm cardboard smell in my room, but none of the eggs hatched, and the ones I opened were just rotten.

We finally sold The Dutch Mill and rented a house north of Disko that Daddy had remodeled for Dr. Seward, the eye doctor in North Manchester. Doc's property, as we called it, was back a long gravel lane. The two-story house had a fieldstone porch that wrapped around the front and side. Two majestic catalpa trees stood in the front yard, filled with clusters of white flowers in the spring and long brown beans in the fall. We had woods, fields, and ravines all around us and a barn and silos nearby, all good places to play. Mom and Daddy remodeled the inside of the house completely. I became accustomed to hearing the whir and whine of the circular saw and the tap, tap, tap of the hammer, three taps to a nail. I liked the smell of fresh wood and sawdust.

Mom painted the new kitchen a cheery yellow, a color she had always longed for, and we girls helped coat all the new louvered closet doors with linseed oil. Because Grandma was still living with us, she had her own little room downstairs. As long as she lived with us, she would show people her room and proudly say, "Now, this is my abode." We still had our watchdog, Nip, but Mom also let us bring home a new puppy named Spunky.

As wonderful as it had been living in The Dutch Mill for my first twelve years, it was exciting to move on. The Dutch Mill had actually become a little rundown. The store had stood empty for years. The gas pumps were unused, and the white paint was peeling. It was beginning to be a little embarrassing to say that The Dutch Mill was my home.

It must have been a big job to sort and move all of our stuff, but all I remember is suddenly being in the new house, away back by itself in the country. Because we had crossed the county line to get there, we were forced to change schools.

We moved just in time to start school at Laketon Elementary. I went into the sixth grade, one big class of forty students, which met in an airy second-floor room with a semi-circular window filling one wall. It was in the old brick part of Laketon School that my dad had attended as a boy when the Gearharts lived in nearby Ijamsville. Sixth grade was my best year because I liked the teacher, Mr. Faudree, and as the new girl I was immediately the center of attention. The popular girls like Kristy, Patti, and Jocelyn invited me to their homes and to slumber parties.

My first Laketon boyfriend was Patrick Wray, who combed his hair down into a curl on his forehead. Later, Keith Cole began writing me love letters on little scraps of paper, and I wrote him back. We "went steady," and he gave me rings. Then Ted Little began writing to me. They both said they loved me forever, but it was just childish talk and puppy love. We all lived in the country and hardly ever saw each other outside of school.

Actually, I liked to compete against the boys, especially in arm wrestling and running, and sometimes I beat them. I still didn't appreciate my femininity or realize that boys were attracted to what was totally other than themselves, not just someone like them.

We had a small track team in sixth grade that competed with the Manchester schools. I was fast enough to run in the sixty-yard dash and was also on the girl's relay team with Kristy, Nancy, and Kathy Kane. Kathy was the fastest runner.

After one of our track meets, Kathy invited me and some other girls to her home. My mom was going to pick me up from the meet, but wanting to fit in and feel independent, I said, "Sure, I can come. My parents won't care where I am."

When we arrived at her house, down a country road not far from us, I was amazed to see the low-ceilinged shed where she lived, but I thought it was interesting. Her lifestyle seemed so free and easy, like she could do whatever she wanted. Her dad, Joe Kane, was an antique/junk dealer with stuff scattered all around his yard. Before long, though, Mom had tracked me down and said, "Didn't you know we would be looking for you and care about where you were?" I realized they did care and I had no business running off to Kathy Kane's like that.

Daddy and Joe Kane later became odd friends in the antique business. Joe's advice was, "If something doesn't sell, just raise the price."

In November 1963, I remember exactly where I was when I heard that President Kennedy had been shot. I was walking through the gymnasium after gym class when someone told us the news.

My first thought was, *Oh, good. I didn't like him anyway.* My family had voted for Nixon.

But right away I shut up because girls were crying, and I soon realized that it was nothing to joke about. On TV for the next few days, nothing was on except news about Kennedy and Lee Harvey Oswald. I was awed by the drama of it all, but disappointed that my TV shows weren't on.

Not long after that, we watched the Beatles on *The Ed Sullivan Show* in January 1964. All the girls fell in love with the Beatles and the other rock groups that soon followed. We bought teen magazines and cut out pictures for our walls. We read about the stars' likes and dislikes. We decided which Beatle was our favorite—I liked George Harrison because his birthday was February 25· like mine.

I loved living at Doc's place where there was so much room to play and explore. At school or when I visited my cousins in Akron, I learned about flirting with boys, talking on the phone, and getting cokes at the drugstore. But at home, it was a different life. I was reading horse books at the time like *The Black Stallion.* As I ran down the lane or rode my stick horses, I felt like I was racing the black stallion himself.

Mindy often felt left out. She wanted me to play with her instead of reading books all the time. But we did play together in the fields and woods and around the corn cribs, imagining we were soldiers or explorers. Daddy got us several kinds of balls and a badminton set. I played basketball, baseball, or kickball whenever I could. I also got a better telescope that stood on three legs and was almost as tall as I was. I could actually see the little line that is the ring around Saturn, the dots that are Jupiter's moons, and the fuzzy oval of the Andromeda galaxy. When I got my telescope, Mindy got a new bicycle so we would be equal.

Behind the corn cribs, a long hill sloped down to a deep lake. One morning we heard that a man named Anderson had apparently drowned in the lake. It was like a real-life mystery in our own back yard. Had he been murdered? Where was the body? I stood at the top of the hill as skin divers tried to find the body in the ninety-foot-deep lake.

I wanted to watch with the telescope, but Mom said, "I don't think you'd really want to watch them drag that body out. It isn't something you'd want to see."

After a few days, they found the body, and I did look through the telescope, but I couldn't see anything clearly. They said that Anderson had probably been drinking and fell out of the boat. No crime or mystery, but it was still great drama for a few days. I also used the story to scare Mindy with the idea that Anderson's ghost still floated about.

Because Grandma was living with us, she helped mom in the bright new kitchen and laundry room, doing dishes, cleaning up after meals, and doing chores that probably should have been mine. She seemed to like feeding the dogs, making them a hot meal at night by adding water to the crusty bits in the skillet, and then adding bread crusts and scraps.

Grandma and Mom never wasted anything. They cleaned out the jelly jars by putting their bread on a fork and wiping the jar clean. They never threw away leftovers, however small, but put them in Tupperware containers and stacked them in the refrigerator. Daddy would get leftover potatoes fried for breakfast, or leftovers would show up in his lunch or as a side dish for supper.

Daddy was very gracious to let his mother-in-law live with us, but sometimes she would get on his nerves. Grandma would be up early, putting away dishes and banging around in the kitchen. Daddy liked to linger over breakfast and sit quietly in the morning before going to work. He would say to her, "Can you be quiet? Can't you do that later?!"

The other thing he couldn't handle was advice on how to move furniture. I learned to never tell a man how to get a chair or dresser through a door, like Mom or Grandma sometimes tried to do: "If you would just turn it around and on its side...." It's better to leave a man alone and let him figure it out himself!

We didn't have air conditioning in our house, making it extremely hot in the summer in our upstairs bedrooms. We put a box fan in the window, but even then, Mom said it was better to have the fan pull the hot air outside than having the cooler air blow in on us, so we never felt a cool breeze. When it was really hot, we slept downstairs on the floor and put wet washcloths on our stomachs to cool us off.

Moving on to the seventh grade was a big change after the happy times at Laketon. The three Manchester elementary schools and Laketon Elementary sent their seventh graders to Central Junior High in North Manchester. We entered that blocky red brick building with wide eyes and great expectations. Once we were inside, all of the old social groups were thrown together, shaken up, and allowed to settle again into a brand-new society, much like a giant science experiment. New leaders and popular kids rose to the top, and the rest of us soon found out where we stood in the social strata.

During the first weeks of school, we Laketon girls looked over all the new Manchester boys to pick out who we liked. My best friend was Patty Gushard from Laketon. She was pretty, with long, straight hair, nice clothes, and a bold, silly personality.

She said, "I like Dave and Bob."

I found out right away where I fit into the social crowd and picked out the boys I liked. I said, "I like Randy and Danny." Both Randy and Danny were in the trumpet section of the marching band with me. I got Danny Beck to notice me.

That fall, the school had a dance called a mixer to get us all acquainted. It was time to shave my legs and wear pantyhose for the first time. I needed Mom's help with this, but I was also embarrassed at the same time. Feeling awkward and uncomfortable at the dance, the boys and girls stood around the edge of the gym floor until the braver ones began to dance. Eventually Danny came over and asked me for a slow dance. As we danced, I asked him if he liked to be called Dan or Danny, which was all I could think of to say. He said he preferred Dan. And that was just about the whole conversation.

Later in the school year, we had a square dance. I thought it was fun because everyone was forced to dance and we constantly traded partners, but most kids thought it was a little corny. Again, I danced with Danny.

After a short time, Danny gave me his dad's Masonic Lodge ring, so we were "going steady." We sat together at some high-school basketball games, never knowing what to say to each other. It was so boring that we finally broke up.

Jimmy Allen from Disko visited us for supper sometimes at Doc's place because he was still our friend, but I began to see him in a new light. Also, when I saw him in Akron with my cousins, Lynn and Shelly, he seemed to be talking and smiling like he was interested in me as a girlfriend. I always thought he was cute, so, why not?

I told Mom, but right away she said, "No. He is too old for you. He is not right for you."

And I realized she was right.

About this time, we began hearing about a crisis in Vietnam that grew into a war. The only person I knew who went to Vietnam was Jimmy Allen, and not long afterward, he was the first person I knew who died in Vietnam. He was killed in a helicopter accident.

CHAPTER 5

My best friend, Patti, lived in a ranch-style house with modern furniture and no clutter. Both of her parents worked outside the home. I thought they were rich and sophisticated. Patti had her own room, with a coordinated bedspread and curtains and a closet full of clothes. When I stayed at her house, we played ping-pong in the basement, called boys on the phone, and walked to the drugstore in Laketon for a Coke. For lunch, we cooked thin cheeseburgers as big as the skillet.

My home seemed common next to hers, but I was proud of my parents. My dad was letting his hair grow long, 1960s style, with dark curls forming around his ears and down his neck. He looked like Al Pacino. Patti liked to come to our house because my mom was so caring and our home was so casual.

Sometimes Patti asked me questions about God because she knew I went to church. I knew a lot about Christianity but had put off making a commitment to God myself. Our pastor, Roy French, was a dairy farmer with a white farmer's forehead above a dark tan face. He spoke very simple messages each week, but he always ended with an invitation to salvation. I sat toward the back of the church, sometimes watching the clock to see how long I could hold my breath, but I was still convicted of my need for salvation. I was convinced of what I had to do, but I was afraid to make the move outside of the pew into the aisle and down to the front. We called it "going forward," and it was a public confession of our decision to follow Jesus.

I would especially be convicted whenever an evangelist would visit our church. My favorite was Stephen Manley. He looked like an evangelist with his shiny black hair slicked back and his piercing dark eyes, but even though he was passionate, he didn't raise his voice or put on a show. He was totally genuine and spoke directly to my heart. But I had learned that if I resisted the convicting thoughts until after the meeting was over, once I got outside in the fresh night air and people started to talk and joke, it would leave. Mindy had a more tender heart, and she was born again a year before me.

It happened for me on April 11, 1965, Palm Sunday, when I was thirteen—the night of the Palm Sunday tornadoes. The day had begun hot and humid, but as we got ready for the evening service, dark clouds rolled around and the wind picked up. My mom was to be the speaker that night. We went quickly up the steps into the church as the wind slammed the door shut behind us with a bang. We could hear the storm rushing outside, but we went ahead with the service. Halfway through, the lights went out, so we lit candles and carried on. Mom's good preaching, along with the roaring of the storm outside, put everyone in a reflective mood. The small crowd all ended up at the altar to pray.

An old farmer who attended church irregularly stood up and said, "I've come here for many years, and I just want to repent of my shallow life and my sins. I want you all to forgive me. I'm not too old to repent and make a fresh start."

That broke the ice. I said, "I want to give my heart to Jesus and be born again tonight." I made my commitment that night, and I left the church knowing it was settled.

We woke the next day to hear that there had been tornadoes that night, the worst in Indiana history. One hundred thirty-seven people had been killed. It was especially bad near Kokomo, where a town called Russiaville was almost completely flattened. To the north, it was just as bad. The scariest picture in the papers was the tornado near Goshen, with the twin funnels looking like a black giant on two squat legs coming right down the road. With tornadoes to the north and tornadoes to the south, we had been safe in the Disko Methodist Church, and I was born again. At the same time, tornadoes held a fascination for me, and I always wanted to see one.

Now that I was in junior high, I was picking up new information from the other kids and trying to put together an understanding about sex. I used a scientific approach, taking the things I'd overheard and researching them in the encyclopedia until I had it figured out. Mindy and I came to the realization about sex at about the same time. We walked into the kitchen to approach Mom and Daddy.

Mindy asked, "How many times did you have to *do* that before you got us?"

Daddy answered truly but wisely, "Just once for each of you girls."

That answer seemed to satisfy Mindy, but I knew there was more to it than that.

I looked at the *Better Homes and Gardens* baby book where Mom had recorded our birth weights and the dates when we started walking and talking and so on. At the front of the book, it showed pictures of the woman's body with the baby inside. I was horrified.

"How does the baby get out?" I asked Mom.

She said, "Well, everything changes and stretches. It's painful but a mother soon forgets the pain with the joy that the baby is born." She said that she had natural childbirth, and that was the best way.

I said, "I don't care. When I have a baby, I want them to give me a total anesthetic and just wake me up when it's all over."

That summer we graveled the road that Daddy had blazed up the hill. One night we decided to camp there overnight. We took Nip along and packed food, blankets, and supplies. We cooked supper over the fire and got our camp ready, but it was hot, the mosquitoes started biting, Nip started barking, and we just decided to go home.

We still spent a lot of time on the farm that summer, thinking about the house we would build, having picnics, picking raspberries, and building fires. By the end of the summer, we had the loan of $19,000 to build the house.

That fall I started eighth grade. Patti and I had been best friends all summer, spending time at each other's houses, helping together at Vacation Bible School, and going to Long Lake to swim and meet boys. She made everything more fun, helping me with social skills, and I sometimes wondered why she wanted to hang out with me because I was so quiet and boring. But when eighth grade started, she was spending more and more time with a new boyfriend, Mike, so we went our own ways. Without Patti, I started hanging around with the more academic girls that year. My social life was weak, but I was still always on the lookout for boys.

My biggest crush that year was on my eighth-grade history teacher, Mr. Corson. Mr. Corson walked smartly in front of the class, nicely dressed with a shirt collar that snapped shut under his tie. Most of the girls fell in love with him and were jealous of his petite wife who taught eighth-grade health just down the hall. Everyone liked him as a teacher because he made history interesting. He loved the Civil War, telling us stories and having us do special projects. I illustrated my projects with pictures and diagrams to please him and get bonus points that he handed out for extra work.

One day, when I was supposed to be in band class, I was coming back from the bathroom, and he saw me in the hall.

He asked, "Where are you supposed to be right now?"

"In Band," I said.

He gave me his charming smile and said, "Oh, a fugitive band student!" (We had been studying about fugitive slaves in History.)

I just giggled, happy that he was talking to me alone.

Later, on the back of a big history project I had done, he wrote a note saying he was proud of me as a student and hoped I would consider the important field of education as a career. The note said that for a "fugitive band student" I did fine work.

I was thrilled to get a personal note from Mr. Corson. I imagined that it was more than just an academic note, though he probably didn't realize I was in love with him. But there's no future in a teenage crush on a teacher, and the next year we moved on to high school and the Corsons moved to Chicago.

By that time, we were actually building our new house. The cement slab was poured on top of the hill at the very place where we used to have picnics, the place where we looked out across the valley and talked about building a house someday. The impossible dream was coming true. Mindy and I walked around on that cement slab and said, "This isn't big enough for a house."

Daddy marked off the rooms, showing us where we would each have our own bedroom. "This little square can't be big enough for a bedroom," we insisted.

But it was just an optical illusion. The living room was thirty feet long, and our bedrooms were plenty big enough when they were done. Daddy worked on that house every spare minute, and he did it all himself, except for the brick-laying. Mom was by his side, staining wood, painting, and cleaning.

Our new house was beautiful when it was finished. It was a weathered brick ranch-style with dark brown trim. We girls put our two square handprints in the cement sidewalk next to the date, 1966. The view out my bedroom windows was of the woods and the valley toward Twin Lakes and Disko. We couldn't see another house from any of our windows.

Daddy said, "I own all this land around us, so nobody can build a junky house or pull a trailer in beside us."

I decorated my new bedroom with pictures of rock groups and a poster of the earth rising behind the moon. I loved the house that Daddy and Mom had designed for us, the wall of bookshelves, the swinging saloon doors in the bathroom, the dark walnut woodwork, the fieldstone fireplace, and the real brick floors in the kitchen and living areas.

We mounted the Civil War sword and rifle on the wall and set the antique clock on a shelf. These were our first three antiques dating back to The Dutch Mill, but we soon filled our house with more. Mom had begun going to house auctions while we lived at Doc's and started bringing home furniture and small items for our house. She persuaded Daddy to go with her just once, and before long they were going together, buying truckloads of antique furniture and boxes of miscellaneous stuff. Mom bought an antique guidebook with descriptions and prices of antiques. It's the only book I ever saw Daddy read besides the *TV Guide*.

Together they rebuilt, restored, and refinished things until our house became an antiques-and-collectibles shop. We sat on antique chairs at an antique table. We ate from old dishes, and Mom cooked with antique kitchen items. Our bookshelves and old cupboards were filled with glassware and collectibles. The whole house was a conversation piece.

Outside, Mom and Daddy spent many hours turning the woods into a yard. They hacked away at the underbrush and then pushed the lawnmower over rough ground to mow the scrappy grass. They mowed such a big area that when they got to the end of it, it was time to start over again! Mom did most of the mowing with a shiny red face and tan shoulders.

Daddy had an endless battle with the lane, forever filling potholes, adding gravel, and cutting back weeds and bushes. After a heavy rain, the road up the hill washed out in places and had to be filled in. When it snowed, sometimes we couldn't even get up the hill. But it was beautiful in all seasons. Oak trees arched over the road like a canopy in the summer. Wildflowers carpeted the woods in the spring and brown leaves in the fall. Snow outlined the trees in winter like a black and white photo.

We moved into our dream house in 1966, just in time for me to enter the ninth grade at Manchester High School. The schoolwork was easy for me. I read all the textbooks, did my homework on time, and continued to get good grades. The hardest part of school was the social aspect of it—how to look good, fit in, find a boyfriend, and keep my weight under control.

Shortly after I started tenth grade, I was asked out on my first real date in a car. Terry Martin had just turned sixteen and had his driver's license. He came up the hill in his parents' Volkswagen bug one nippy fall evening and walked up to the door wearing a heavy red plaid CPO jacket. Terry's family had a dairy farm about fifteen miles away on the other side of Manchester. He talked about milking cows and chopping silage—so many chores that he didn't even have time to eat supper.

But he loved to dance. Our usual date was to go to the Swing-In at the Huntington YMCA basement. They had live bands every Saturday night, and I quickly learned a few simple dance moves to keep up with Terry. After the dance, we stopped for a sandwich, since Terry hadn't had time to eat earlier, and we got back home early before his curfew. I was so happy. I had a date every week, and we were soon going steady. I felt secure with him, and we were comfortable with each other—even though we didn't have a lot of sparkling conversations. I was quiet, and he was a simple country boy. I overlooked his big ears and his loud laugh.

Terry taught me how to play pool at his home where the pool table filled their living room. On cold winter nights, we ice skated on a patch of ice in their field. My ankles wobbled around, but it was fun. For my sixteenth birthday in February, his mom made me a cake with the words *Sweet Sixteen* written in purple icing. Terry gave me a heart-shaped necklace.

The next summer, we were still going steady, usually dancing each weekend and then spending Sunday together. After church on Sunday, I would join Terry's family as they towed their boat to Salamonie Reservoir or Lake Wawasee, ate a picnic lunch, and then water skied all day. Having a steady boyfriend had lifted my spirits and helped me lose some weight over the winter. By the summer, I was looking good in my two-piece bathing suit and was eating very little. I still thought I needed to lose a little more weight, however, so I just picked at my food on our picnics. A little pork and beans, a little sandwich, not much milk or anything fattening like mayonnaise.

Terry's family taught me to water ski. They were very patient. I wore a life jacket and a life belt, so I was halfway out of the water before we started. I weighed little more than a hundred pounds, so I shot right up when their speedboat took off. At first I fell a lot, but they circled around to pick me up, encouraged me, and let me try again. Before long, I was a great little skier and even tried skiing with only one ski like Terry did. I got a nice tan, and the exercise took even more weight off. I was pleased with myself.

My junior year started out fine. I liked my school picture that year, but Mom said that I looked a little gaunt. She thought I was getting too thin.

I said, "Don't worry. I'm fine. I look just right."

But on October 18 of that year, everything changed. Terry said he wanted to talk. I thought that maybe he wanted to talk of marriage someday. Instead, he said that we should just be friends and date other people. I was devastated. I had no idea that was coming. For the next few months, I thought he would change his mind and come back to me. What did he see in Rita, anyway? I got up the courage to call him once but nothing changed. I cried every night for over a week. All the songs I heard seemed to remind me that I had lost my boyfriend: *For Once in My Life* by Stevie Wonder, *I Heard it Through the Grapevine* by Marvin Gaye. Nothing was fun anymore, and I settled into a depression. For months I struggled like this. In my English class journal, I wrote about how I just wanted to lie down somewhere and go to sleep or disappear. I wrote poems and lamented in my journal about the boy-girl dating situation and life in general.

I liked other boys, but nothing ever worked out. I went to basketball games, dances, and Mike's Café, but nothing special happened. Mom dutifully drove me to events and picked me up, doing what she could to help me out. She was also praying for me, but I didn't know it at the time.

I especially began to like a boy named Roger. I flirted with him, but he was quiet and intellectual, very hard to catch. We did finally go out on a couple of dates and went to the prom together. I told him I really liked him, but I think I may have scared him away because he backed off and I was right back where I started.

By my senior year, I was gradually coming out of my shell. I observed the popular girls and concluded that guys liked girls who were silly and acted dumb, so I tried to act sillier and worked even harder on my flirting. I developed more friendships, moving into more popular circles, but I was still desperate for a boyfriend who I could be happy with.

Toward the end of my senior year, my life changed again. I met my Prince Charming, my knight in shining armor, just like in the movies. It was March, the weekend of the senior fish fry. I had made some vague plans with some friends, ever-hoping for my big break with the boys. In the hallway before math class that morning, Jeff Barnett, the popular athlete of the school, came up to me and asked if I would go with him on a double date. Without thinking, I asked, "Really?" in disbelief. I thought he was joking.

We were in senior math class together, where he sat diagonally in front of me, but we never talked. I would admire him in class because he was popular and had such a muscular, athletic body. He said, "Yeah, I want you to go with me to a movie with Joe and Christine."

I stammered as I remembered my plans, but then said, "Sure, I'd like to go."

My other plans weren't important compared to this. It was too good to be true. After class I looked up Mindy so I could tell her my good news. That night at home I told Mom. I explained to her all the background and details, who Jeff Barnett was, and why this was so big for me.

That Friday we went on our double date to see *The Magic Christian* in Warsaw with Joe and Christine. The movie was about the Beatles and had a stupid storyline, but who cared? I was sitting next to this handsome guy! On the way home, we were sitting in the back seat because Joe was driving. I started out on the edge of the seat and then sat back farther to be more comfortable. Jeff thought I was making a move, and he bent over and kissed me. I was thrilled. But after I got home, I realized that for someone popular like Jeff, this was just a typical date for him, one of many, and I would never hear from him again.

The next night was the senior fish fry. All the seniors had to participate, breading the fish, assembling the dinners, or serving in some other way. I knew that Jeff would be there, but I wasn't sure how to act or what to expect. I decided to be nonchalant, telling myself not to expect anything at all. Most of the boys were on the fish breading crew, getting their hands right in with the fish and the batter. Sometime during the evening, Jeff left the crew, tracked me down, and asked if he could take me home. Of course, he could! I was dumbfounded. I knew we had something going on.

Jeff took me home, went in the house, and met my mom and dad. Mom was friendly as always, doing her best to make everyone feel comfortable and at ease, but Jeff was a little scared of my dad. Daddy had little to say to people and didn't care about being socially acceptable.

After that, Jeff wanted to see me every week, practically every day. He was finishing spring baseball and would come to the house after practice, all sweaty in his baseball clothes. I was proud that my new boyfriend was such an athlete. He played four sports in high school—baseball, basketball, track, and football—and excelled in them all. I had watched him play basketball when he was the leading scorer. I saw him hit a grand-slam home run in baseball. I knew he was so good in football that he wanted to play in college.

I liked everything about Jeff. He was flamboyant and easy to talk to. I liked his strong, take-charge personality. And he seemed to like me just as well. He had admired me because I was quiet, and he said he had actually been intimidated by me because I was one of the smart kids. Mom had prayed for me that I would find someone I would be happy with, and God had answered her prayer.

I went to Jeff's home south of North Manchester to meet his parents. His dad, Dalton, worked for NIPSCO, the gas company. He loved sports and fishing. His mom, Ruth Ann, was a teacher's aide and liked to knit and crochet. His brother, Brad, had just gone off to college in Montana, and his sister, Tana, was a junior in high school. Jeff's mom kept their country home clean and tidy while his dad maintained a perfect yard with the John Deere lawn tractor. They had a new truck and a new yellow Olds Cutlass, much different than the vehicles I was used to. My mom had a Rambler, and my dad had a work truck full of tools and saw horses. Before the Rambler, we had a Ford Galaxie. And our lawn was a woods.

Jeff's parents always gave me a big glass of Pepsi with ice when I was in their home. We would sit together in the living room where they played with their brown Dachsund dog, talking baby talk to it. I didn't really care to be around dogs and I was shy around people, so I listened, answered questions, smiled, and drank my Pepsi.

Jeff's mom asked after one of my visits, "She seems nice, but does she ever talk?"

"Sure, she talks to *me*. She's just quiet," he said.

I floated through the end of the year on a cloud. Jeff and I were seniors, on top of the world. On Awards Day, I got the valedictorian scholarship from Manchester College for being ranked number-one in our class. Jeff got the Hall of Fame Award, along with his best friend, Randy Straka, for best athlete of the year.

High school ended with graduation, standing in a circle around the gym, holding lighted candles, singing "Bridge over Troubled Waters." It was wonderful because my boyfriend was there, as well as my mom, sister, grandma, and even my dad! Daddy was nervous and uncomfortable, but I was proud he was there, looking handsome with his long hair and a stylish brown double-breasted suit.

After graduation, I got my first job at the Heckman Bindery in North Manchester. The bindery took worn-out books and put new bindings on them for libraries and schools. The books started at one end of the factory, rolled along in stacks on a conveyor of metal rollers past workers who each did a specific job, then came out at the other end, all boxed up and ready to go.

I was a back-stripper. I stood in front of a wall of cubby holes filled with various sizes of cardboard strips. My job was to find the correct size of cardboard, or back strip, to fit along the spine of each book. Because I had never had a job before and had barely worked at home, the days seemed extra long. The summer days were muggy, but inside the bindery, I had to wear a sweater because of the freezing air conditioning. Because Jeff came to see me most evenings, I was up late at night, but I still had to be at work by seven in the morning. I could barely keep my eyes open as I watched the clock and longed for noon. For lunch I always had a carton of milk and half a sandwich, since I was still watching my weight, and I never ate honey buns from the vending machine during break time like the career workers there. I worked at the Heckman bindery two summers at $1.65 an hour, the minimum wage at that time.

My mom had started working at Peabody Seating Company in North Manchester to help pay for my college tuition. Tuition at Manchester College was three-thousand dollars, and my scholarship was only for one-hundred dollars, plus there would be room-and-board costs because I planned to live on campus. At Peabody's, she was a drill-press operator—a dirty, strenuous, man's job, lifting metal desks and chair legs onto a drill press to be stamped into shape. Working at Peabody's certainly didn't make good use of her talents. She didn't complain about her work, but she came home tired and dirty, then had to fix supper and do whatever else needed to be done. I'm sure I didn't appreciate all that my mom did for me. I was more concerned about my weight or getting a suntan or thinking about my boyfriend.

> *And what is so rare as a day in June?*
> *Then, if ever, come perfect days.*
> JAMES RUSSELL LOWELL

Mom used to quote these lines of poetry on perfect June days. One such June day, only three months after our first date, Jeff asked me to marry him. We were taking a walk, as we often did, in the field behind my house and sat down by a big rock. When Jeff asked me to marry him, I didn't know what to say. We were just out of high school, and he was moving way too fast, even though I did want to marry him more than anything else in the world.

I gave him a sensible reply: "Wow, that's a big decision. We need to think about it for a while." So I made him wait.

I started school at Manchester College, and Jeff went off to Indiana University in Bloomington, three hours away, determined to make it big in football. His vision was clear and focused. Although he didn't have a scholarship, he was going to try out for the football team as a walk-on. He was filled with confidence and determination. I was going to college because I loved to learn and I knew I had the ability to do something great. I just had no idea what it was.

Manchester was a cozy little school, with tree-lined sidewalks and historic brick buildings, as well as newer structures. I lived on campus in a new co-ed dorm so I could experience college life to the fullest, but I missed Jeff so much that it was hard to enjoy myself. I went home most weekends and every day I wrote a letter to Jeff. The highlight of each day was checking my mail slot to see if I got a letter, which I usually did, with an artistic IU symbol in red marker in the upper left corner. He wrote long romantic letters telling me how much he loved me. The girls on my floor were jealous of me with my steady boyfriend. I slept in a huge peach-colored T-shirt covered with paint stains that Jeff had worn at his summer painting job. They all knew that my boyfriend had worn this shirt, and I proudly wore it in front of them.

Jeff was very busy playing football, trying to keep up with schoolwork. He did make the freshman team and got his scholarship, just as he planned. His picture was in the Manchester paper: the small-town boy who made it big. He was in the paper again when he scored a safety against Ohio State to win the game for the freshman team. He was a fierce linebacker and was getting the coaches' attention.

I was able to go to some of the games with Jeff's parents, who were as proud as they could be of their son. Jeff had fulfilled his dad's dream of seeing a son succeed at sports. Standing in that yawning IU stadium on a clear Saturday afternoon, part of a shouting crowd of thousands, and watching Jeff down there on the field, was just plain thrilling. After the game, we would go down on the field to get up close and personal. He wore the cream-and-crimson uniform, number 28. After one of those games, on October 31, 1970, in the courtyard of McNutt Quad, I told Jeff I would marry him.

CHAPTER 6

In January 1971, my life made yet another turn. At Manchester College, we had a January interim to be used for intensive study of one subject for one month. I took the class called The Faith of Israel. In those four weeks, I was immersed in reading much of the Old Testament, along with a textbook about the Jewish faith. I attended classes each day taught by a Hebrew scholar. He told us that the first five books of the Bible were not written by Moses, but were actually written much later by different groups of writers based on oral tradition. The same was true with the Old Testament books of history and the prophets. In other words, he was saying that the Bible was not divinely inspired. My life-long faith was being questioned. When I talked to Mom about it, she grew concerned for me.

During the last week of this course, some old friends from the Disko church invited Mindy and me to go to a crusade in Fort Wayne to see Nicky Cruz. I had read *The Cross and the Switchblade* in high school, and I knew that Nicky Cruz was the gang leader who had been totally changed by God through the ministry of David Wilkerson in New York. That story had left an impression on me, so I wanted to go see Nicky Cruz.

When we got to the Scottish Rite Cathedral in Fort Wayne, people were crowding the doors to get in. We flowed in with the crowd, but we were unable to find a seat until an usher said to Mindy and me, "Come right down to the front. We have a couple of seats there."

Nicky Cruz came out on the stage, clearly a man who had been a fighter. He had a strong, compact body, quick reflexes, and a passionate look on his face. He spoke with a Puerto Rican accent, but his message was clear: Jesus Christ had changed his life. He had a horrible childhood that had left him filled with hatred. He had even wanted to kill David Wilkerson when he first met him, but now he was standing before us telling of God's love.

Nicky Cruz gave an invitation for anyone who wanted to be born again or needed ministry to come to the front. Counselors streamed in from the sidelines. Our friends from Disko joined with a counselor, so Mindy and I just stood there waiting. At the time, I was thinking that my Christianity did not have the strength that Nicky Cruz was talking about. Because we were right there in the front, a female counselor came up to us and asked if we needed anything.

I said, "Sure, we'd like to talk." The woman took us into a back hallway, and we sat down on some steps. She said her name was Lillian, and she began to review the Four Spiritual Laws with us. I stopped her at the second law and said, "I already know all that. We're Christians, but we just don't seem to have any strength. Our church doesn't seem relevant, and it's like we live a different life at school. I don't share my faith with anyone. I get excited and inspired at a revival or a youth retreat, but as soon as it's over, I just feel weak again."

She smiled and said, "I'm not supposed to say this at this meeting, but what you need is the baptism in the Holy Spirit. That's where you will get the power to change your life. In the book of Acts, the disciples were filled with the Holy Spirit after Jesus left them and then they had the power to change the world."

It sounded interesting. "Where do you go to church?" I asked.

She replied, "My husband, George, is the assistant pastor at a little church that meets in a house in Claypool."

A church that met in a house sounded even more intriguing. "We live just down the road from Claypool," I said. "Maybe we could go there tomorrow morning."

She said, "My husband usually speaks there because the pastor travels so much, but tomorrow the pastor will actually be there. It's a little pink house right beside the water tower."

After that conversation, Mindy and I were ready to give it a try because our spiritual hunger was so great. I had had long talks with Jeff about God and life and truth. We would jog around the college track at night and sit on the bleachers discussing these things.

I had said to Jeff, "How do we know what the real truth is? Maybe the Amish or Old Order German Baptists are right. Maybe you just have to make a total commitment like that to be happy."

I felt that the Methodist church wasn't giving me what I needed. And I knew the Holy Spirit was important. I had just been reading an old book about the power of the Holy Spirit that Mom had picked up at a sale. Mindy had her own concerns—she was only sixteen and was afraid she might be pregnant. So, we were willing to try something new in the hopes of getting some help.

We stood on the doorstep of that little pink house the next morning, a cold Sunday in January, not really knowing what to expect. Once inside, we saw two small adjoining rooms full of folding chairs in rows, with little room left to move about. At the far end was a young man playing a guitar behind a makeshift podium, which was actually just a dresser drawer set on end with a board on top.

"That's Jerry," I whispered to Mindy. "He went to high school with me!"

As I looked around, I noticed some people I'd seen at the crusade the night before. Everyone raised their hands in worship, singing simple songs of reverence while Jerry led with the guitar, then they clapped to joyful songs of praise to the beat of a tambourine. We felt welcome there even though the people were preoccupied with their worship. We found seats and just took it all in with eyes wide open. This was not at all like our Methodist church.

After much singing and what sounded like people quoting the Bible, a tall lanky man, who looked remarkably like Billy Graham, walked stiffly to the front with an obvious limp. He was the pastor, Dr. Hobart Freeman, and he commanded everyone's attention. He had a Ph.D. in theology, and he was teaching the last in a series of messages on the book of Revelation. He spoke for an hour or more about the end of the world and the new heavens and the new earth. He spoke with the conviction that all these things were going to happen just like the Bible said. After the meeting was over, we talked with some of the people and then left the pink house knowing we would be coming back.

That night I returned with Mom. The singing was even livelier than earlier that morning, and the message was about faith. This church believed that God would really answer their prayers if they just believed. The pastor told stories of people being healed of sickness and being protected in storms by commanding the winds to stop. He believed that his leg would be healed from the polio he had had years before. We had never heard such stories before. At the end of the service, we went to the front for prayer, and Mom just broke down to the floor crying because she was so worried that Mindy might be pregnant. She cried out for God to help us.

After this meeting, I believed that I had finally found what I had been looking for. After my weak experience in the Methodist church and the disturbing ideas I'd heard at college, this church's teaching had the ring of truth. It not only restored my original faith, but it went far beyond that, adding experience, relevance, and emotion. Looking back, it was as if I had been divinely guided there for answers, right when I needed them most. Why else had Mindy and I ended up at that Nicky Cruz meeting, in the front row, singled out by that counselor, and directed to this church, right when we faced family problems and right when my faith was wavering?

As soon as I got home, I called Jeff and told him all that had happened. I had hoped that he would be as excited as I was. He was at least partly prepared for my phone call because two months earlier he had become a Christian in his dorm room after talking to a Campus Crusader, Norm. Most of the athletes who lived in McNutt Quad were proud and disrespectful to Christians like Norm. They liked to make fun, throwing light bulbs down the hall after him. But one day Jeff decided to listen to Norm, and he gave his heart to Jesus.

As I told him my story, though, he was worried that I had gotten involved in something strange—meeting in a house, miracles happening—and he warned me to be careful.

I said, "You'll just have to come and see for yourself."

But then I was worried, too. I wasn't sure I could picture this athlete fitting in with the people in the little pink house, even if he was a Christian.

The next time Jeff was back home, he visited the church with me, and he liked it immediately. We all soon received the baptism in the Holy Spirit, Jeff in the little chapel at Indiana University and Mindy, Mom, and I at home. Mom was the first to receive, singing in a different language after asking for the baptism in the Holy Spirit at home. Mindy and I spoke to the pastor's daughter after a church meeting, and we also received. We began going to all the meetings that we could, although Mom was still involved in the Methodist church. Jeff went with us whenever he was home from school and all during the summer. The teaching we received there was clear and relevant. It was changing our lives.

That summer I worked at Heckman Bindery, and Jeff worked with the house painting crew. But our goals were changing, and together we wanted to find out God's will for our lives. I decided to transfer to Indiana University so that we could be together. Jeff would continue to play football and major in social work, hoping to become a professional football player and be a witness for Jesus in that way. I was learning that God considered a woman's role in the home as a wife and mother to be the most noble and worthiest calling. I wanted to be the best wife and mother possible, so I decided to major at IU in home economics.

I loved being at Indiana University that fall. My room was on the girls' side of McNutt Quad, where Jeff lived. McNutt was on the northern edge of the campus by the football stadium so I had to walk a long way to class, up and down hills, which kept me in good shape. I got up early for my 7:30 A.M. Foods class, but I didn't mind the walk past the oval track and the field house, past historic fraternity halls, then down to the ivy-covered limestone buildings of the central campus. I wore my frayed bell-bottom jeans, a flannel shirt, a T-shirt, and hiking boots. My hair was long and straight.

At lunchtime I would sometimes rendezvous with Jeff to give him a biscuit or a muffin I had made in my Foods class. We walked together through the old sprawling Union Building to Dunn Meadow outside where hippies were throwing frisbees or playing guitars. We both liked the scenic wooded campus with its ivy and limestone. There were also new buildings full of classrooms and modern high-rise dorms. It was like a city in itself.

Jeff continued to do well in football, and I went to all the home games. In the winter, we watched some Bobby Knight basketball in the new field house. But our primary focus had been put on God. Jeff was even wondering if he should go into ministry. We attended Christian meetings on campus and sometimes even in Indianapolis.

One day I noticed a Jesus symbol on a classmate's notebook and asked , "Are you a Jesus freak?"

"Yeah," she said. "Praise God!"

"That's cool. I'm a Jesus freak, too," I said.

Whenever we went home, we visited the little pink house church in Claypool. We found out that Mindy really *was* pregnant, and in September, Bryan James was born. Our new faith helped Mom and all of us to welcome this little baby. It took some patience for Mom and Dad, Mindy, eighty-year-old Grandma McQuiston, and little Bryan to live together in the same house.

One day in December 1971, we were in church, on the front row, right where Jeff liked to sit, about a foot from the podium. After his message on faith, Dr. Freeman reached out his long arm toward Jeff. Jeff started to shake his hand, but Dr. Freeman just moved his hand over to Jeff's head. He prophesied to him that night that God was going to use him "like a razor's edge, to cut away error and unbelief in many of My people." He said that God resists the proud and uses the humble, and that was why He was going to use Jeff. When he heard these words, Jeff was weak and shaking. It was a defining moment for him. Jeff knew that God had an important purpose for his life.

We finished our sophomore year of school at Indiana University and were married in June 1972.

CHAPTER 7

No price is set on the lavish summer;
June may be had by the poorest comer.
And what is so rare as a day in June?
Then, if ever, come perfect days.

JAMES RUSSELL LOWELL

In keeping with the earthy, back-to-nature seventies, we were married in my own back yard under a simple white trellis decorated with daisies picked from the field. I made my own white wedding dress. Mindy was my maid of honor in a long, pale blue dress, and we both wore floppy, wide-brimmed hats. Our wedding colors were blue and yellow. Jeff looked extra sharp in his tuxedo with striped vest and old-fashioned tie, as did Randy Straka, his best friend and best man. Patti's daughter, Bridget, was our pretty little flower girl. Daddy gave me away, handsome in his suit and tie. Mom wore a lacy dress, and I could tell she was so happy for me.

A group of young people from the church at Claypool sang as we walked down the aisle, and Steve Hill sang "The Wedding Song" while playing his guitar. The assistant pastor, George, performed the official ceremony, speaking for a long time it seemed, and after this simple service, we were man and wife. As the crowd filed by, we smiled until our faces felt creased into place, hugging and shaking hands with family members, old church friends, new church friends, and a handful of high-school friends. Wedding cake and blue punch were served from our patio. All the while during the reception, Jeff sat by me, holding my hand, telling me how happy he was that we were married. He was so romantic.

For our honeymoon, we drove to northern Michigan for a week in a cabin in the woods. I cooked hamburgers and beans and other picnic food as we spent our first days together as husband and wife. We traveled over to Lake Michigan on a windy day to watch the waves crash into the shore, and then we went fishing on a small lake, taking pictures to preserve this special time together. We later found out that all our honeymoon pictures were lost, because we somehow ruined the film.

The first night, however, we only drove to the Holiday Inn in Grand Rapids. What a strange feeling it was to be married! Jeff checked us into the hotel, awkwardly referring to me as his wife, while I sat in the car wondering where we would eat. I was hungry, but I didn't want to eat too much and look fat. We ate at Burger Chef.

We returned from our honeymoon to the little home we had rented in North Manchester, which was called "the dollhouse." A box of food had been left there by our new church friends to help us get a good start in married life. The dollhouse was about the size of a garage. It was like a cottage in a fairy tale. A couch opened up to form a bed that completely filled the living room. If I turned around from the stove in the tiny kitchen, I could bend right over the little built-in table to serve our food. It was like playing house.

On those summer mornings, I fixed breakfast, packed three sandwiches for Jeff's lunch, as was customary for him, and then cleaned the house. It didn't take long to get the kitchen and bathroom in order, fold up the bed, and dust our one room. When Jeff came home from work, I had supper ready. The first meal I fixed there was fried chicken, mashed potatoes and gravy, a vegetable, and dessert. I wanted him to know I was a good cook.

It was soon time to return to school, where we lived in a blue-green trailer in a wooded park full of blue-green trailers not far from McNutt Quad. Our new home was about thirty feet long by eight feet wide, but we were happy there as newlyweds. Jeff's football scholarship paid for our housing, and he ate at the team table during the football season, so we didn't need much money. I had decided to quit school because my main interest was my marriage, not pursuing a career. I spent my time taking care of my home and husband and studying on my own.

The little money we had saved during the summer soon ran out, though, so I got a job babysitting for fifty cents an hour to help with our expenses. I cleaned the family's kitchen, made sure the baby was all right, and then watched *Superman* reruns on TV. I had never had a heart for babysitting, even when I had tried it as a teenager. I didn't want to get involved with the kids—I just wanted to see what they had to eat in the house and watch TV.

That spring Grandma McQuiston died after she suffered a stroke. She was eighty-two. I went home to see her while she was still in the hospital and I stayed there for the funeral. I had spent a lot of time with Grandma when I was a child, and for many years, she had lived with us as part of the family. It was sad to think that my mom had lost her mom.

I learned to drink coffee during that trip because I spent so much time sitting around and talking to people, and food and coffee was always on hand. I found out that coffee wasn't bad with cream and sugar, and it made me feel more grown up.

The early seventies was an exciting time to be on a college campus. Beginning in the sixties, my generation had begun to question authority and truth and everything conventional. We were dissatisfied with the establishment—established religion, established government, big business, all of it. We rebelled by letting our hair grow and dressing like hippies with raggedy bell-bottoms, beads, and tie-dyed shirts. Kids tried marijuana and drugs like LSD because they thought it would expand their minds. We listened to loud psychedelic acid rock or to soft folksy songs about love and political issues. Kids had watched their parents search for the good life and apparently find it, living in nice homes with money in the bank, but still not finding happiness in the end. We wanted a cause to live for.

Kids were dropping out of college, taking drugs, and living in communes where they raised their own food and preached free love. They shared everything, from their possessions to their children. They thought this would make life more meaningful, less hypocritical, but it didn't turn out that way. They ended up with drug addictions and children who didn't even know who their parents were.

By 1970, the country was stuck in the Vietnam War, like it was in quicksand. On TV we saw images from Vietnam—helicopters, jungles, fires—and heard about the Vietcong, the Mekong Delta, the Tet Offensive, and always the rising death toll. College students protested the war. They marched and shouted, waving banners proclaiming love and peace, wearing flowers in their hair and peace symbols on their jeans. We were horrified when we heard that some of these peace-loving students were killed at Kent State.

The whole country was divided, and we felt it even in Manchester. Most of the local farm people were patriotic and supported the war, but on the college campus, many felt, as one banner said, "All war is sin." In this time of confusion, when the truth was up for grabs, nothing was considered too strange or weird. Young people wanted to express themselves and believe in something. Some went to the far liberal left, but Jeff and I went to the far right. We found our cause in Jesus. We took a conservative Christian stand even though our church met in a house, believed in miracles, and wasn't afraid to be different.

We were not alone. The Jesus Movement was a growing phenomenon all across the country. People were following Jesus and forming non-traditional churches with contemporary music and meeting styles. They were tired of "established religion" that was not speaking to the needs of the day. The Charismatic movement went hand in hand with the Jesus Movement. In

80

denominational churches, people were receiving the baptism in the Holy Spirit, speaking in tongues, and seeing gifts of healing and prophecy manifested like in New Testament days. These people left, or were asked to leave, their traditional churches, and they formed new charismatic churches that welcomed the free expression of the Holy Spirit.

Our church was part of this exciting charismatic movement that reached across the country and world. Books were written about it, magazines were started, new songs were sung, TV shows were produced, and new churches were planted. People traveled great distances to attend conferences or to find a charismatic church. They listened to taped teachings on their cassette tape recorders and in their cars. Like other charismatic Christians, we couldn't seem to get enough of this new life-giving message.

Being part of the house church in Claypool was like having ancient solid ground under our feet, yet being on the cutting edge, on a new wave. We believed that Jesus truly was going to return to earth soon and that we were part of an end-time army of mature Christians who would be used by God in a special way.

Because of this feeling of urgency, Jeff felt he couldn't put off God's calling into the ministry until a later time. He agonized over it, but he eventually made the decision to quit school and not return for his senior year. Of course, this was a shock to his family and to his coaches. They thought he was crazy, but he stood firm, believing it was the right thing to do. Actually, ever since he had become a Christian, he had lost some of his ferocity as a linebacker. Whereas before he would brag that he had broken an opponent's arm or knocked someone unconscious, now his coaches wondered why he wasn't hitting so hard. He had thought he could be a witness for Jesus as a football star, but once, after he spoke about his faith to a group of junior-high kids in North Manchester, all they wanted to talk to him about was his football statistics, not his Christianity.

We left it all behind and devoted ourselves to our walk with God. Our church had moved from the pink house to a three-car garage. Then, outgrowing that, they decided to move into an old sheep barn near North Webster where they had been having a coffeehouse ministry on Friday nights. It was owned by a burly, whiskery biker named Mack, a former alcoholic who had become a Christian. The people of the church cleaned out the upper level of the barn, filled it with chairs, sound equipment, and a pulpit, and it became our new church. We called it the Glory Barn.

We did have glorious times there. People were coming from all over to our church, hundreds of people. The local people referred to the Glory Barn in derision and tried to spread exaggerated rumors about what we did there. It did attract some odd-ball people who didn't fit in anywhere else, as any movement will, but most of our members were normal, serious-minded young adults.

As we sat under Dr. Freeman's ministry, we saw his genius as a teacher. His theology was as solid as a Baptist minister, but he had the fire of a Pentecostal maverick like Smith Wigglesworth or William Branham. And he had the guts of the early martyrs. His manner was bookish, but he was such a skilled teacher that he kept our attention long enough to teach us biblical theology in terms we could understand. We eventually heard him teach on every passage in the Bible, and he backed up his positions, putting them in the context of church history and current events. All the reasoning was so logical it appealed to our minds as well as our hearts.

After we lived with Jeff's parents for a few months, we found an old farmhouse to rent south of Warsaw. It was a squarish two-story house sided in gray shingles with white trim. We had four big bedrooms upstairs, two living rooms, two extra rooms downstairs, two bathrooms, and a big kitchen—all for just us two people. Most of the walls had been covered with dark paneling, and I made curtains for the long, narrow, old-fashioned windows. The kitchen had black-and-white contact paper on two walls to match the black linoleum floor. Tall white kitchen cupboards offered more storage space than I could fill. Later I carefully painted all of those cupboards in two coordinating shades of green and had a friend put up kitchen wallpaper. We lived there for three years.

Jeff tried his hand at several odd jobs during this time. He worked for the gas company, a horse-trailer factory, a company that polished bathroom fixtures, and also as a bricklayer's hoddy. He worked and studied, knowing that he would eventually be in the ministry. I worked around the house and planted a big garden out back, while studying and enjoying the time alone with my husband. We actually prayed that God wouldn't give us any children for a while, even though our church believed that children were a blessing and taught against the use of birth control.

Dr. Freeman soon started teaching college-level classes on Saturday mornings. We jumped at this chance to learn Old and New Testament theology, Christian ethics, church history, and even Hebrew. Jeff felt that it was preparing him for his ministry, and I just loved to learn. Church history was enlightening. Hebrew was fun as I learned to write the boxy Hebrew alphabet from right to left across the page. We were getting a seminary education for free.

Eventually Jeff decided to quit his job and prepare full-time for the ministry, believing something would open up for him. During this time, we had trouble gathering up the one hundred fifty dollars for rent each month, but we always did, even if it was sometimes late. Our landlord kept chickens on the farm, so we had all the eggs we wanted. We ate a lot of egg-and-cheese sandwiches and vegetables from the garden. Because we had so many bedrooms, we rented a room to a young man in the church for a while and that brought in a little extra money.

Finally an opportunity came for Jeff's first meeting. A relative of a friend wanted him to come to Winamac, Indiana, and start a meeting in their home. They said, "It will be mostly teenagers, and they will only come if they don't have to dress up."

Jeff said, "That's fine. We'd love to come!"

We put on our church clothes and picked up our Bibles and guitar to drive to our first meeting. The kids showed up in jeans and T-shirts to see what we had to say. I led a few simple songs on the guitar and then Jeff preached "from Genesis to Revelation." He had their attention, though, and afterward most of them lined up to receive salvation and the baptism in the Holy Spirit. After that first meeting, we drove there weekly to speak to these teens, bringing home an offering of twenty or forty dollars or so each time. Jeff had now had his first meeting as a teacher.

About this time, we were watching the other young couples at church starting to have their babies. Jeff and I had been married for almost three years. We were used to married life together, and although I had prayed not to have children right away, I realized that I did want one or two. I also realized I probably needed a healing before this could happen. My system had been abnormal since my teenage days when I had come close to anorexia. I asked Jeff to pray for me that I would be normal again and have a baby.

He said, "Sure, I love kids! I want us to have a baby, too."

So, he prayed for me, laying his hand on my stomach. In less than a year, I could tell that a baby was on the way!

Over the next ten years, we went on a wild ride with our church. It was like we had boarded a train that wouldn't slow down and we couldn't get off. Dr. Freeman announced that we would be called Faith Assembly—an assembly of believers with faith as our emphasis. We met in the Glory Barn until it was too full to safely meet there anymore. When the upper level of the barn was packed full, people overflowed to seating downstairs. They would watch the floorboards bend and shake overhead as people danced "charismatic jigs" to the praise songs.

People traveled for miles and then stood in long lines early Sunday morning for a good seat. Of course, Jeff and I always had a good seat because all the young ministers—and there were quite a few—had reserved seats up front.

One day Dr. Freeman announced that we were leaving the Glory Barn because of a conflict with the owner, Mack. We didn't have anywhere else to go, so we met in a big circus tent just north of Warsaw, and later near Goshen. We met in tents throughout that summer and fall of 1978 until we could build our own building. The atmosphere in the circus tent was much like that of the old-time revivals, except that the meetings were not as evangelistic. The messages were fiery, as they led us deeper into our identity and galvanized us as a persecuted church.

By the winter, we had built a huge steel structure in a cornfield on a back road near North Webster that had been donated by one of our members. Now we had a building that would meet our needs. We had big bathrooms, a nursery for all the mothers and babies, and a meeting room large enough to hold two thousand people. It didn't take long to fill most of the seats. It wasn't fancy. The floors were cement, and the walls were bare, but it was ours.

Because Dr. Freeman's teaching was so comprehensive, it soon demonstrated the faults of other churches and movements who "didn't have what we had." We were able to recognize their shallowness or errors and labeled and avoided them. We knew how to recognize cults, but we didn't see our own cultish tendencies. We criticized the denominational churches for their lack of the Holy Spirit and gradually isolated ourselves from most of the others in the charismatic movement because of their lack of doctrinal teaching. We felt we had a "pure word," something worth fighting for. But it got to the point that we would split doctrinal hairs over issue after issue. If someone disagreed with our position, we were willing to forsake friendships to stay with what we thought was the truth.

Also, because Dr. Freeman dealt with what he believed was God's position on every subject, the church became very legalistic. We denied that we were legalistic, of course—because we taught against legalism. We just wanted to please God. Most of us were idealistic young men and women, looking forward to learning the next truth, finding out what else we could do, or give up, to please God more. We believed in principles of right and wrong, but in practice they became unspoken laws. Everyone in the church felt the same way. If not, they just didn't fit in.

People outside Faith Assembly joked that we all looked alike. A typical Faith Assembly family on their way to church consisted of a man, who was probably a construction worker, carrying a notebook and Bible under one arm and a diaper bag over his shoulder. He would be walking with his wife, who would be wearing a denim skirt and carrying a baby, with several other kids in tow. They would drive a van.

We had opinions, based on good logical reasons, concerning women's roles, music, jobs, medical science, government, the military, education, birth control, clothing, sports, holidays, etc., etc., etc. When our kids got older and didn't necessarily share our convictions, all hell broke loose.

But the subject that caused the most controversy was that of divine healing. When I first heard of divine healing, it was like refreshing water. I didn't understand why churches opposed this teaching. Who wouldn't want to be healed? But we took it a step further than most Charismatic churches—maybe even ten steps further. Dr. Freeman taught that it was *always* God's will to heal in response to our faith, and that God would do it without the aid of doctors or medicine. He spoke constantly about faith. He was willing to stake his life and the future of the church on this message of faith and divine healing. It sounded good until a baby died, and some others died who probably would have responded to medical treatment. It eventually led to Dr. Freeman's own death in 1984.

We had backed ourselves into a corner. During this time, several of our young men were traveling and speaking at meetings over a wide area. Jeff was one of them. He had his own weekly meetings and even traveled to Europe and Australia when he was invited. People from all over the world followed Faith Assembly's ministry, buying Dr. Freeman's tapes and books. If you hadn't been part of this movement, you wouldn't understand how a person couldn't just change his mind about these issues. It wasn't that easy to turn a corner and go a different way. We had gradually come to this position, and it took a long time to gradually get out.

The Gearhart Family
Back row (left to right)- Max, Floyd, Dick, Ray, Donald, Larry,
Leonard, Harold
Middle row- Opal, Bill, Grandma Edna, Grandpa Frank, Leo,
Dorothy
Front row- Ruth, Joan, Roger, Sharon

Grandpa Roscoe and Grandma Lena McQuiston with me

Mom and Daddy with Elaine and Mick

Mom and Daddy with Cindy and Mindy

Cindy and Mindy

Me as a Cowboy

Jeff and Cindy

Ready for church with seven kids

The Barnett Family
Back row (left to right)- Joe, Danny, Jeff, Bryce, Vicki, Andy, Aaron, Scott
Center- me and Renee
Front- Rachelle and Audrey

PART 2

"So when did you move into that big white house?"
"Well, we moved there when I was five months' pregnant with Rachelle. She was born in January of 1988. So we moved there in September of 1987."

A mother can usually tell you when something happened in the past by using her children as time markers. The rest of my life falls under headings named after children, because I didn't just have that first baby as a gift from God—I had ten.

CHAPTER 8

Andy was born on a summer night in our upstairs bedroom in the gray farmhouse. It was July 27, 1975. When my labor began that dark early morning, I felt shaky and nervous with excitement. We phoned Marcie, the lady who would be our midwife, and then I rested during those early mild contractions. Late that afternoon, I lay in bed, waiting. Jeff and Marcie had become bored and hungry, so Marcie decided to make an apple pie from the green apples on our tree. Labor was taking its time, and Jeff agreed that an apple pie sounded good. I was hungry, too, but the consensus was that I should not eat while in labor.

I was having my baby at home and had read all about it. The book *Commonsense Childbirth* explained that childbirth is a natural thing, not a sickness to be treated in the hospital. If I understood what happened in childbirth, was prepared, and learned how to relax and breathe, I would be fine. I had sterilized the scissors to cut the cord and had done everything else the book recommended. We were ready. And we had faith that God would bless our baby's birth.

The baby's things were ready, too. I chose the smallest bedroom upstairs for the baby's room and covered the hardwood floor with free carpet samples of all different colors. I filled a dresser with the baby clothes, mostly generic greens and yellows, because we didn't know whether the baby was a boy or girl.

Throughout that summer, I had tended my big garden, getting a nice tan while digging little irrigation ditches down the rows because the summer was so sunny and dry. In the evenings I stood by the fence gazing at the cows in the field, watching the mother cows with their calves and wondering when my baby would come and what it would be like to be a mother.

Earlier that day while I was in labor, I asked Marcie, the midwife, "So, how many babies have you delivered?"

The number she gave us was very small—less than five. "But I've read a lot about it, and I have a lot of faith," she said.

Oh, that's great, I thought to myself. I had thought she had delivered many more babies than that. But it was too late to change anything at that point. Besides, we liked Marcie and her husband.

While Jeff and Marcie were eating their supper and the apple pie downstairs, I noticed that my contractions were getting stronger. I worked hard at relaxing and breathing slowly. Jeff and Marcie finally came upstairs to join me, and within a few hours, the labor became very intense. Marcie wasn't exactly sure when I should push, but when the time came, there was no doubt about it. Andy came out in a whoosh, right into Jeff's hands.

There is no greater joy than the actual coming forth of your first baby. What a relief after the hours of labor that go on and on—and the whole nine months before that! We named our little boy Andrew Lynn. Andrew was a good Bible name, meaning "manly," and Lynn was Jeff's middle name. Baby Andy had seemed big to me, but he looked so small in Jeff's hands. He was six pounds and five ounces, nineteen-and-a-half inches long, and perfect in every way. I sat cross-legged on the bed, looking like an Indian with my hair in two long braids, while they cut and tied the cord. Marcie rolled Andy up tight in a blanket.

That night Andy slept in the bassinet right beside my bed making little chirping noises like a bird. From the moment of his birth, all the instincts and love that come with being a mother flooded through me. We were a family.

Dalton and Ruth Ann came to see Andy the next morning, and my mom stayed with me a few days to help out. Dalton said to Jeff, "It just seems like the whole world stops when you have a baby, doesn't it?"

"You know, you're right. It does seem like that," we agreed.

Andy was born on a Sunday night, and by Friday we were ready to go to Jeff's Winamac meeting. We never stopped after that—to Faith Assembly on Sunday morning, Sunday evening, and Wednesday evening, and to Jeff's weekly meetings at Winamac, New Whiteland, and Greensburg. We stayed up late, eating in people's homes and in restaurants. I packed the diaper bag, and we just went wherever we needed to go. If Andy cried, I would breastfeed him almost anywhere.

Not that it was easy. The baby seemed to take up all of my time. On top of everything else, I was growing tomatoes and squash in the garden, and we were learning Hebrew at the church. I sat down with Jeff by the garden one evening and felt like I was going to cry.

"I feel like I just can't get anything done with this baby and the garden and all," I said.

Jeff tried to encourage me. "It's all right. You're doing fine. Just take it a day at a time."

Jeff started taking pictures of Andy the morning after he was born. Andy with Dad, Andy with Mom, Andy with Grandpa, Andy in the bassinet, in the little bathtub, in the swing, Andy awake, Andy asleep. As he grew older, we documented every event and every activity. Andy looking in the mirror, Andy in the chair, Andy with his toys, and later, Andy on the pink plastic horse, brushing his teeth, opening gifts, eating cake.

When Andy was only two months old, we took a trip to Colorado. A friend of a friend had said we could stay in their condominium for free. I had been to Colorado once before as a teenager, when Elaine and Riley took Mindy and me and all their kids there. At that time, I had a fear of motion sickness and that in itself made me sick when I traveled. I often drank from a bottle of PeptoBismol and was fairly miserable for most of the trip. But I still loved the mountains. Everything was so Western out there.

Jeff and I took off for Colorado before dawn in our yellow Cutlass with Baby Andy asleep in my arms. There were no laws at that time about seat belts and car seats. We just had Andy in a flimsy plastic baby carrier, lying on the back seat. We made it to Colorado in two days. October in Colorado was gorgeous. Deep crayon-blue skies were spread overhead, not like the watercolor blue of Indiana. The mountainsides were marbled with dark green pines and clusters of yellow aspens. The air was so clean and still, I drew a deep breath when I looked across the wide valleys to mountains in the distance. When we drove through the mountain passes, there was snow on the ground. We stayed a week in the condominium in the woods with Baby Andy, tromping around in the dry leaves and sightseeing, then we drove all the way back home.

We lived in the gray farmhouse a while longer, but Andy never slept in the bedroom I had fixed for him. We kept him in the crib in our bedroom for almost a year.

I seemed to know how to be a mom by instinct, with a little help from my mom and the *Better Homes and Garden's* baby book. And I wasn't alone. There were lots of new moms in our church, meeting in the nursery to feed babies and change diapers, keeping toddlers quiet with toys and Cheerios.

Before Andy was a year old, we stopped at Marcie's house one day. "Guess what?" we asked.

Marcie answered right away, "You're going to have another baby!"

"How can you tell?" I asked.

"Oh, I can just tell," she smiled. "And it's about the right time."

She was right. After waiting three years for Andy, I was already going to have another baby.

Until then I had my hands full. Andy was not strong-willed or out of control, but he was a wiry, brown-eyed sprite, a normal boy who liked to run and play. When he slowed down, he liked to stand and look at the world, with his right thumb in his mouth and his left hand on top of his head, twirling his reddish brown hair until it formed a little bald patch there.

I was getting used to being a mom. Our life was fairly simple, centered around the church, going to meetings, and studying theology. At naptime I listened to the classes again on tape and took notes. We didn't watch TV. We didn't bother with celebrating holidays.

We were one of the few who made it to church to hear Dr. Freeman's first official teaching about Christmas. It was December, and it was snowing. We slid to church over the country roads in our Cutlass—without snow tires. Eleven inches of snow were on the ground by the time we got home. Only five or six people made it that day to hear about the pagan origins of all the Christmas traditions and why we therefore shouldn't celebrate it. But it was no problem to give up Christmas and the other holidays. We just wanted to please God.

AARON

By January of 1977, I was ready for my second baby to arrive. We decided to have our baby in the Goshen Hospital with Dr. Unziker, a Mennonite doctor who believed in natural labor. We figured my due date was February fifth. Each night I made sure that everything was in order, bag packed and house clean, so that I could be ready to go when the time came. Each night I took a bath, looking over the top of my watermelon stomach, and wondered if that would be the night.

We were snug that winter in a little apartment south of Warsaw. It was a middle unit in a long building of five apartments, with rustic wood siding and a cedar shake roof. We had shag carpet in the bedrooms and the sunken living room. The kitchen and dining room had flooring that looked like bricks. It was modern and cozy compared to the drafty old farmhouse. Our front window looked out onto a little pond with a bridge that arched out to a tiny island. The apartments were called Rancho Cost-a-Plenty.

It had already been a snowy winter, but on January 26 it started to snow and didn't stop until about a foot of snow was added to the ground. Then the temperatures dropped far below zero and the winds began to blow at thirty to fifty miles an hour. We looked out the window and watched the snow blowing sideways and the drifts piling up in graceful curves around the house. We decided to turn on the little black-and-white TV someone had given us, and soon realized we were in the middle of a blizzard. We hadn't known it was coming because we didn't watch the TV or pay much attention to the news. The wind blew for days and the wind chills were dangerous. Nobody could drive anywhere for a while, and I wondered what would happen if I started into labor.

When we finally dug our way out to the highway several days later, it was like nothing I had ever seen before. Snow plows had chiseled a path through the drifted roads. Only one car at a time could pass through in some places, the snow like walls on either side. I tried to keep my appointments every week with Dr. Unziker, driving about an hour north to Millersburg on snow-covered highways. I actually went three weeks past my due date, getting ready each night in case labor started.

Finally on February 26, I felt contractions, so we made the trip to Goshen Hospital. It turned out that I wasn't really in labor, so we went back home and I cried because of the wasted trip and the discouragement of having to wait so long. But early the next morning, we drove to Goshen again through the sleet and the rain, and Aaron was born at ten o' clock that morning. Although Aaron was born in the hospital, Jeff was with me, and the birth was natural. As soon as Aaron was born, healthy and crying, they wrapped me in a heated gown. What a luxurious feeling! We named our little boy Aaron Matthew, Bible names meaning "exalted" and "gift of God."

Mom came to stay with me a few days and help with the new baby. Aaron was a roly-poly baby with brown eyes and brown hair. He was always happy, always smiling. Big brother Andy was fascinated with his new baby brother. He hovered over Aaron as he lay in his little seat so he could look at him and touch his face. Aaron didn't form the habit of sucking his thumb like Andy had, but he got me in the habit of rocking him to sleep, even when he woke up in the middle of the night. I tried to get him to stop by letting him cry it out one night, but I couldn't stand it after a while. I gave in and rocked him back to sleep.

With two babies now, I didn't travel so much. Jeff went alone to his Tuesday night meetings at New Whiteland. Whenever I did go, it meant spending most of my time in the back bedroom nursery and it also meant getting home after midnight. The church met in the house of Fred and Susie Wagner. It was still fun to go because Susie cooked southern home-cooked meals for us after the meetings. She fixed Swiss steak on rice, spaghetti, barbeque sandwiches, and for dessert, luscious Red Velvet cake or cheesecake.

It was Fred and Susie who let us borrow their motor home to drive to Montana. Jeff's brother, Brad, lived in the northwest corner of Montana near the town of Troy, not far from the Canadian border. We decided to drive there with ten-month-old Aaron, two-year-old Andy, and our third baby on the way. We were young and adventurous. We were ready to go with $150 in cash and a motor home packed with food, clothes, and baby stuff.

We headed west at sunrise, rolling across the country, state by state. I loved the feeling of entering the unknown, finding out that each state had its own charm. I followed along on the map as the towns and countryside changed. The sky got bigger, the trees disappeared, and the dirt changed colors. At night I could see the whole sky as I'd never seen it before.

Andy and Aaron wouldn't stay in the back of the motor home in their seats, but they always ended up front with us, leaning against the round console between our seats. At that time there were still no laws about seatbelts and car seats. And I wasn't about to go sit in the back because I felt queasy in my early pregnancy. We stopped at campgrounds for the night and prepared most of our own food.

After two long days of traveling, the motor home broke down in Butte, Montana. We seemed to have no power going up hills, so we stopped at a filling station and they said it was the water pump. Butte was a cold, gray mining town on a wind-swept plateau. Snow flurries were in the air. We sat for a whole day in the motor home waiting for the new fuel pump to be installed. It cost us $120, but we had no choice but to pay the money.

We finally arrived at Brad and Diane's house, situated down a gravel road in a beautiful wilderness setting among the mountains. *How great it would be to live like this*, I thought. A stream gurgled under the wooden boardwalk that led up to the front door of their brown cabin, and smoke drifted from the chimney. It was the kind of place where a person could wear plaid flannel shirts, jeans, and rugged coats all the time. The cabin smelled of smoke from the wood-burning stove used for heating and the cook-stove in the kitchen. The Carpenters' album was playing on their stereo, lending a lonesome but good feeling to their home.

We stayed with Brad and Diane a week. Jeff loved being with his brother, whom he hadn't seen since Brad had left for college in Missoula years before. Brad was a westerner now, a loner. He worked as a firefighter, cut his own wood, hunted, and fished. Diane was a librarian at the school, a very feminine contrast to Brad, but doing fine in the wilderness.

We fixed big meals of spaghetti or chili and laughed at Andy and Aaron as they made a mess with their food like little pigs. Andy, in his furry tan coat, played outside with the cats, or followed Brad around, or rode with him in the truck. We took walks with the boys during the day and listened to Brad and Diane tell moose and bear stories in the evening.

On the long trip back home, Aaron started pulling himself up to stand next to things, and when we got home, he took his first steps, the earliest of all the kids, walking at about ten months. He always wanted to be first and best at everything.

JOSEPH

We still lived at Rancho Cost-a-Plenty when Joe was born in the spring of 1978. We had just gotten over the Blizzard of 1978, which started almost a year to the day after the Blizzard of 1977. Being pregnant kept me warm that winter. As I grew heavy and awkward in the ninth month, the spring weather was cool and comfortable. The month of May is the best time of year to have a baby, I think. Aaron was toddling around that spring, and Andy was just under three years old.

It was an exciting time for Faith Assembly. We had left the Glory Barn and were meeting in a circus tent that spring and summer, with little protection from the wind and the rain, the heat and the cold. Our nursery was a row of vans where mothers could go with their babies, and we used porta-johns for bathrooms.

We decided to have our third baby at home with a "real" midwife, Kelly, who had nursing experience and had been at many home births. We had a better understanding of childbirth now and everything went fine. Joseph Edward was born late in the evening of May 15, my biggest baby at eight-and-a-half pounds, with a light complexion, blond hair, and blue eyes. Joseph was Grandpa Dalton's middle name and means "God adds." Edward means "guardian of prosperity."

So now we had three sons. If I was feeding Joe, and Jeff was holding Aaron, there was no one left to chase after Andy. It seemed as if there was always one too many little boys who needed something—a regular three-ring circus. We had two in diapers by day; all three in diapers by night.

But three little boys were cute when lined up like three little stair steps. Whenever I bought them new pajamas or hooded sweatshirts, Andy ended up with green, Aaron red, and little Joey got royal blue. People gave us clothes, and we handed things down from one boy to the next. Andy's furry tan coat with its hood was worn by each of the boys in turn.

Norm Wheeler, our landlord and neighbor, liked to tease us: "Don't you kids know where babies come from?" People thought it was cute to say things like that.

Our answer was, "Yes, we do. But we believe that children are a blessing!"

And we did believe it. Jeff loved to get his picture taken while holding his three sons. He liked to lie on the floor and wrestle around or have his sons crawl all over him, like a bear with its cubs. For my part, I gave motherhood my whole effort, believing it to be the most worthy cause. I was on my feet most of the day cooking, doing laundry, and looking after the boys. I stopped to nurse the baby and sat down at naptime, still listening to taped messages from church, taking notes, and studying. I tried to keep the little apartment tidy, but the sunken living room was always covered with toy trucks and baby toys. What was the point of stowing it all away in a wooden box at night only to get it all out the next day? I reasoned.

It was becoming our custom to take a trip somewhere after each baby. When Joe was about a year old and I was expecting another baby, we went to Sanibel Island in Florida. We took Baby Joe with us and left Andy and Aaron with Grandma and Grandpa Barnett. It was springtime in Indiana, but as we drove south, it was like going forward in time. More and more green leaves and flowers appeared until we came to full-blown summer in Florida. We stayed in a condominium with breezy pastel rooms not far from the beach. It was all so tropical and luxurious to me because I had never been to the ocean before or even seen a palm tree. I wore a blue maternity swimsuit as we took long walks down the beach looking for shells. The fair skin on little Joe's shoulders and nose soon turned pink while we worked hard to keep him from eating sand. We fell asleep to the rhythmic sound of ocean waves at night.

I was expecting another baby in July, so we moved out of the apartment, which was getting a little crowded, and into one of Norm Wheeler's new duplexes about a block away.

RENEE

Our fourth child, Renee, was born in July 1979, a few days before Andy turned four years old. The new duplex was larger and better suited for our three boys and growing family. Jeff loved the big attached garage, and I liked the big yard, although it had only a few tiny trees. As usual, our long front room was always cluttered with toys. When I had to show the landlady to the back of the house one day, I kicked a path through the toys like I was swatting away flies. The playpen, baby swing, and high chair were becoming permanent pieces of furniture in our home.

I went into labor at the end of July during the week of the Kosciusko County fair. We called our midwife, Kelly. She thought the baby was coming face-up because of the way it felt when she examined my stomach and because of the way the labor tended to speed up, then slow down. From her experience with face-up births, she explained that it might be very painful and difficult. We prayed that the baby would turn before it came out and then just waited. Kelly left for a while that evening to go to the fair with her family, but she returned just in time to watch Renee come forth with ease, no trouble at all, face down and normal. She was small, only six pounds and twelve ounces, which had made it easier for her to turn and come out the right way.

We had our first girl, finally. We named her Eva Renee, which means "giver of life" and "reborn." We planned to call her Evie, but as soon as we saw her, we knew she was Renee. She had a few pink spots on her forehead, which later faded, and a mop of black hair. She looked like me.

Our friends loaded us up with pink baby girl clothes and girlish accessories. Everyone was so happy for us. We kept Renee in the playpen so that she would be safe from her older brothers —who either adored her or were at least curious about the new baby. She grew round and contented while I was busier than ever, constantly on the run, trying to keep up with my family.

Joe was only fourteen months old when Renee was born. Soon after her birth, we had a real scare. While we were eating chicken almondine one day, Joe began to choke in his high chair. We saw that he wasn't able to breathe, so I yanked him out, patting him hard on the back, praying for the food to come out. I was amazed at the thoughts that passed through my mind while time seemed to stand still. Jeff took over, and in desperation, he stuck his finger down Joe's throat and pulled out an almond sliver. Joe began to gasp and breathe again. He was fine. We believe that God saved Joe's life that day, and we were extremely thankful.

Renee was pretty in her little dresses and pink outfits, dark hair in sweaty curls on her neck, but she wasn't the baby for long. When she was only about five months old, I realized that I was going to have yet another baby. I had breastfed the boys until they were a year old, but I had to wean Renee early because I needed all the energy I could get. I felt like I was forcing her to grow up too fast to make way for more.

I heard about a mother who was asked how she divided her love among her many children. She answered that she didn't divide her love, she multiplied it. I did my best to multiply my love to include all that God gave me.

The yard at the duplex wasn't fenced in, so I constantly checked out the windows to make sure the little boys didn't get out on the road. I watched one winter as the boys, dressed in primary-color-block snowsuits, were building a snowman in the front yard. It was just one big ball, as big as they could roll, with a little ball on top for a head with two rock eyes. Andy and Aaron posed by it for a picture. They were so proud of what they had made, but I laughed because it was so cute, not the traditional three-ball snowman. When Aaron saw me laughing, he thought I was making fun of it and kicked it down. I felt bad, but it reminded me of the lemonade stand I built as a little girl at The Dutch Mill. Mom had explained to me the reasons why she thought it wasn't a good idea and that I wouldn't make any money, so I got mad and tore it down. Same thing.

Renee was one year old, just learning to walk, during the summer that my next baby was due.

VICKI

It seemed like little Vicki started life with one strike already against her. Not only was she a middle child, number five out of ten, but she was born premature. She was due to be born just thirteen months after Renee in August 1980, but she came early. She weighed only five pounds and four ounces.

That summer was hot, but thankfully we had air conditioning. A family from the church, the Barettas, lived in the other half of the duplex, and they were expecting a baby about the same time. Mrs. Baretta was a cleaning whiz. When I crossed over to her side of the duplex, her kitchen always smelled of Pine Sol, and everything was in its place. She had two kids, and I already had four. Our kids played together in the back yard, and we compared notes on our pregnancies. One thing that concerned us by the end of the summer was the whooping-cough epidemic in our church. It seemed as if all the families were getting it.

A few weeks before my due date, I had just finished gathering all the items for the birth, when I woke up one morning and felt water leaking. I went ahead to the grocery store, but after going down a few aisles, I realized more water was coming. I left my cart, went home, and we called the midwife. She said that maybe the leaking would stop, but if it didn't, we should pray that the baby come soon because there was danger of infection, especially after three days. Two days later, my labor did start, and Victoria Kay was born late at night on August seventh. Victoria means "victory," and Kay is my middle name.

It was an easy delivery because Vicki was so tiny. She had reddish hair and spidery arms and legs. We knew that she would grow and fill out, but I dressed her in fuzzy sleepers instead of dresses to make her look fatter. Another nurse-midwife came by to visit me soon after the birth. She looked at Vicki, and, aware of the whooping-cough epidemic around us, she said, "She's so little," in a caring nurse's voice that sounded like she was really concerned.

Sure enough, about three weeks later as we sat around the table, one of the boys started to cough. Soon they all had the telltale whooping cough, including little Renee. I decided I had to protect my baby. I was determined to keep her in the bedroom, because all she did was sleep and eat—and I would not allow any of the older kids to go in for three or four weeks until the cough had run its course. Maybe a child crept into the bedroom once or twice, but the plan worked. We kept Vicki isolated for weeks while the kids coughed until they threw up.

I was worn out caring for everyone. Then I developed a suspicious hacking cough myself, and I wondered if I had the whooping cough, too. I couldn't quarantine myself from Vicki. Whatever it was, I did eventually get over it, and Vicki was fine. She continued to grow and gain weight, as if nothing had ever happened.

In the middle of this time of sickness, we were invited to go out to eat in Warsaw with another couple from the church. As we walked into the restaurant, we noticed a few other friends from church who had apparently chosen the same place to eat that night. Then we walked into a big room, and it was filled with over a hundred friends from Faith Assembly. It was a surprise baby shower for us! They presented us with enough money to buy a dishwasher, because we obviously needed one with five kids.

We loved these people. We felt a very real camaraderie with all the other young couples who had growing families like ours. Jeff was well-liked by everyone because he was friendly and because he was a leader in the church.

The "ringleaders" of the party pulled us to the front of the crowd to interview us as if we were on TV. They put a microphone in front of me and asked, "Why do you think your husband should receive the Father of the Year award?"

I was speechless. Not only was I naturally shy, but spending all my time at home with the kids hadn't helped me to develop my social skills. I couldn't think of anything clever to say—or even anything at all. Jeff looked at me, waiting.

After a minute of silence, the interviewer said, "Maybe we've got the wrong guy for this award!"

Everyone howled while I just grinned, still with nothing to say. They gave the microphone to Jeff and asked him why I should be the Mother of the Year. Because he was used to speaking in front of groups, he easily complimented me in front of everyone. It was just one of my most embarrassing moments, I guess.

Even as we celebrated the birth of our fifth child with our friends, I thought of little Vicki at home and prayed that she would survive. Of course, she did survive—we all did. But I felt like I was at the end of my strength sometimes and longed for just a day alone.

We would occasionally get a babysitter or one of the grandmothers to watch the kids so we could go shopping in Fort Wayne. We didn't have the chance to shop very often, so when we did go we needed lots of things. Once we stayed overnight in a hotel on one of these trips instead of going straight home. I told Jeff, "I would love to just stay in a hotel for a day or two and put jigsaw puzzles together in complete peace and quiet."

During this time, my dad started to remodel a storage barn he had built beside his home in the woods, intending to build a house for us. He had already built a house at the foot of the hill for my brother, Mick, and his wife, Jo Etta. His dream was for Mindy and me to have homes of our own on his property, too.

Mindy's life had taken a different turn from mine, although we both had big families. When her son Bryan was two years old, she left home to live in a communal arrangement with several other teenagers from Faith Assembly in a big rambling house in Winona Lake. It was organized and overseen by a woman in the church who had two teenage children of her own. They remodeled this big three-story house, painting it light blue with black-and-cream trim. Depending on your opinion of the place, it either stood out like a sore thumb or it was a place of beauty among the other old houses along the lake. Mindy gave me a tour of this house, showing me the bedroom assigned to each teenager, and explained their job assignments. They worked, pooled their resources, and went to church together. This was the 1970s, when such an idealistic communal idea wasn't quite so unusual, so Mindy and Baby Bryan moved in. She met a young man there, who seemed to be a spiritual and intelligent person. After a while, they decided to get married because it seemed to be the right thing to do.

After they had several children, Mindy realized that her husband was not as spiritual as we all had thought. And although he *was* intelligent, he had no common sense. Mindy's life was miserable as they moved from house to house to follow her husband's changing plans and ideas. He never settled down to provide for his family. Mindy had nine more children after Bryan: Jessie, Abby, Ben, Jed, Havilah, John, Joel, Lynisa, and Cecilee. Her husband was abusive to them, especially to Bryan.

With very little money, Mindy always managed to decorate her home in charming ways with antiques and creative items she had made. She made sure the kids had what they needed. With God's help, she got them through every crisis, always listening and counseling them. I often wondered why her life was like a nightmare next to my fairy tale, but I still don't have the answer to that question.

Daddy did build our family a house in the woods, just like he had dreamed. After it was finished, he said he probably should have torn down the old structure and started from scratch, but instead he poured a foundation under it and went from there. The ceilings were low and the walls weren't at right angles by doing it this way, but we were excited as we watched it take shape. He bought old doors from auctions to put in the house— doors that were made of solid wood and better for being old. He built everything with our family in mind, like stairs with a gentle slope and deep steps so the kids wouldn't get hurt falling down the stairs. The big square kitchen, with room enough for a ten-foot table, had quarry-tile floors and handmade cupboards. He added lots of windows to give us a good view of the woods, lots of bedrooms, a convenient laundry room, two bathrooms, and two porches. Mom helped to stain the woodwork and to paint. It was to be our dream home. We would pay three hundred dollars a month for ten years, and it would be ours.

By December 1981, it was ready to move in. There was no siding, no garage, and lumber and tools filled the front porch, but the inside was ready. It was the middle of a snowy winter, but we were anxious to move in. I was expecting my sixth baby.

CHAPTER 9

DANNY

Moving day was in December, and it snowed six inches of fresh snow. The trucks barely made it up the hill. All of our possessions and our five little kids were unloaded in the cold and carried into the house. Never mind the junk on the front porch or the unfinished outside walls—we stacked everything in piles in our new house, and we were home to stay. The woods looked like a winter wonderland, with snow outlining every branch and frosting every bush. Smoke rose from the chimney of my mom and dad's home not fifty yards away.

We finished moving just in time to set up beds, find sheets, towels, and pajamas, and get five kids to sleep that night. I was three months' pregnant—and very tired.

I woke up in the middle of that first night and looked out the window. The snow had stopped falling, and the moon was out, so bright that the trees cast blue shadows across the snow. I went from room to room, looking outside from every angle at stark outlines of trees, soft piles of snow, the very air tinted blue. I felt so blessed and safe to be there in that house, built with my father's love, with my sleeping children all around me, and the wonderful silent night outside. I made Jeff get up and look, too.

It snowed almost every weekend that winter. The wind blew at our house set on the hill, bringing its chill right through the walls, which didn't have that extra layer of siding. To keep warm, we loaded up our wood-burning stove, which sat on a fieldstone hearth in front of a whole wall of fieldstone. It was the center of attention in the living room, usually surrounded by wet snowsuits and gloves laid out to dry like a day's wash.

Springtime came, covering the hillside in wildflowers. The kids loved to play in the woods and fields or down the hill where my brother, Mick, and Jo Etta lived. Their three sons, Chris, Jeremy, and Courtney, were ever-ready playmates. I was always busy as usual with cooking, housework, and babies, but the older kids often walked over to Grandma and Grandpa Gearhart's, where Mom took them in and gave them Kool-aid and special attention.

With the coming of nice weather, my dad began building a garage for us. On June 26, Daddy was working on the garage, not knowing I had gone into labor early that morning. We didn't tell him, either. I walked around the house and spoke to him like it was a normal day. He paid no attention when Kelly the midwife came to help with the birth. Late that sunny afternoon, Daniel James was born upstairs while my dad hammered and sawed outside the window.

After everything was over, and Danny was wrapped up in a little blanket, Jeff took him outside, where it was a warm eighty-two degrees, and presented him to my dad. Daddy didn't know what to say in his surprise.

"Yep. You better take him back inside," was all he said.

Danny was a beautiful baby. He was round, happy, and smiling, with wisps of light brown hair that stood up down the middle of his head like a mohawk haircut. Daniel means "God is my judge," and James is my dad's middle name.

What a time we had getting to church with six kids, three times a week, forty minutes each way! But we went faithfully, whatever the weather. On Saturday mornings, I fixed food for our Sunday meal, something like chili or spaghetti. Or I would cook a chicken, take the meat off the bones, and use it for some kind of casserole. I made sure that our clothes were all clean and everyone had a bath Saturday night. On Sunday morning, I dressed all the kids, fixed toast or cereal for breakfast, packed the diaper bag, and put lunch in the crock-pot or in the oven on timed bake. After a few minutes to get myself ready, we were off. By the time the meeting was over and we had driven back home, it was already early afternoon when we ate our Sunday dinner. Everyone felt they were starving by then so it was a good thing food was always ready.

Sunday afternoons were a time for rest, but by five o'clock, we regrouped and drove to the Sunday night meeting. The church was at its height at this time. People saved their seats on Sunday morning for the packed house on Sunday nights. The numbers spoke of the church's success, but its weaknesses were there, too, if we were able to admit them. We got home late at night, had a bowl of cereal and went to bed. On Wednesday evening, we did it all over again.

That fall it was time for Andy to start school—my first child in first grade. He went to Laketon Elementary, where I had gone and my dad had gone before me. I fixed chocolate milk and cinnamon toast for Andy's breakfast and drove him down the lane to meet the bus.

About this time, we bought a blue four-wheel-drive Ford van from Mr. Duncan, a friend from Faith Assembly who had moved up to Indiana from Louisiana.

"What kind of gas mileage does it get?" we asked.

"Oh, about ten miles a gallon or so. In the winter, it just depends on how deep the snow is."

But at least we could go anywhere and there was more room for our family. John Dilley painted stripes on it that stretched the length of the van and then bent up to the roof. Andy dubbed it the "spic-and-span van" when washed, waxed, and shiny. We made a big down payment to Mr. Duncan, leaving a balance of three thousand dollars.

When Danny was a few months old, Jeff was invited to go to Germany, Switzerland, and England for a five-week speaking tour in churches related to Dr. Freeman's ministry. The Fussle family made all the arrangements. Heinz Fussle had lived in Warsaw for many years making Christian films. His sister, Hildegard, and his mother also lived in Warsaw, and his brother Helmut lived in Germany and Gunther in Switzerland. They arranged this trip, and I was invited to go, too. How could I do it with my family? But how could I pass it up? Danny would be ten months old when the trip was planned for that spring of 1983, Vicki was only a year and a half, and although we had tried our best to space out our children without birth control, I was already expecting another baby. Andy was only seven.

Several families and the grandparents offered to babysit for me. They encouraged me to go and not to worry. I was excited as I told my dad I was going to get to see the Germany that he had loved so much and that was home to our ancestors. We decided that I would go for the first half of the trip to Germany and Switzerland, and then return by myself while Jeff went on to England. Of course, I would take Baby Danny along. We bought a camera, a slide projector, and boxes of film to document this trip of a lifetime.

And it *was* the most awesome trip of a lifetime, despite some problems along the way. I got my passport in Chicago, just hours before the plane left. I held Baby Danny in my six-month pregnant lap for much of the nine-hour plane flight. I didn't pack enough warm clothes for the April weather so I got a cold after walking in the rain the first day there. I suffered jet lag, fatigue, fever, and fits of coughing. When it was over, I cried part of the way home, flying alone without my husband, holding ten-month-old Danny the whole flight, and still coughing.

But it was still the most awesome trip! Everyone loved Danny with his chubby smiling face and his hair sticking straight up. I was fascinated by everything European. Helmut and Gunther took us sightseeing. I was amazed by the Swiss Alps. I ate Swiss chocolate and real Swiss fondue. I walked through a walled medieval town. We drove through tidy German towns, uncluttered by trash just like my dad had said.

At one point we drove south through the Swiss Alps, stayed overnight, and crossed into Italy. That night, I thought how strange it was that I was in Switzerland, my baby was with Gunther's wife hours away, and the rest of my family was on the other side of the world.

When I got back home, I was utterly exhausted and facing two-and-a-half weeks alone, six months' pregnant with six little kids. At least the coughing and sickness left right away. The kids had their own adjustments to make after being split up for such a long time. We all came back together and tried to carry on. After dealing with everyone else's needs all day, I longed for some peace and quiet. The kids just craved my attention, especially little Vicki who needed some security after moving from family to family while I was gone. As much as it seemed as if God had made a way for me to go on this trip, it had still been hard for Vicki. She clung to me, not wanting me to leave her sight. It wasn't easy for her to get over this feeling of insecurity.

I decided that no one could sleep in the bed with me at night while Jeff was gone. It was my only time alone, and I needed my sleep. The kids had their own beds, and they needed to stay there. Shortly after we all returned home, a spring storm woke us up with loud, booming thunder and flashes of lightning. Vicki came running into the bedroom, wanting to crawl in bed with me. But I knew that if I let her, she would want to sleep with me every night, so I made her go back to her own bed. I felt bad, but I was just so tired. I didn't realize how much she needed me.

After two-and-a-half weeks, Jeff came back home with his own stories to tell. His briefcase had been stolen with his billfold, passport, plane tickets, and three thousand dollars' worth of offerings, the result of all his speaking on the mainland. It was quite a story. In order to replace his passport and airplane tickets, he had to convince the stiff, unfeeling British who he was. As God's will would have it, our good friend Tim McNeal had just landed in England and could vouch for who he was. So they replaced his passport and tickets, but he still had to replace all his notes by memory for the meetings in England, and he still lost the three thousand dollars, which was earmarked to pay off our van.

But when Jeff returned home, Mr. Duncan said, "Forget it. Consider the van paid in full." It was a lesson in trusting God no matter what happened.

That summer our seventh child was born.

SCOTT

Scott was born just thirteen months after Danny on July 21, 1983. Andy was not quite eight years old when Scott came along as number seven. The details are fuzzy in my memory, but it was either a Sunday or Wednesday night when I went into early labor. We discussed with the midwife whether we should all go to church, just send Jeff and the kids, or all of us stay home. I can't even remember what we decided, but I do know that Scott was born after midnight in the same upstairs bedroom of the house in the woods. We named him Scott Alan. Scott means "a man from Scotland," and Alan means "handsome." Everyone in the church had been using all the biblical names, so we wanted something different. Scotty had bright blue-green eyes and light hair.

We had a riotous house full of kids now. We kept Baby Scotty in the playpen for protection, but the playpen was the worse for wear. The plastic was torn and the sides were bent down, but it still offered some safety from rowdy older brothers, toddler Danny, and little girls who wanted to mother the baby.

After each birth, I soon got my figure back because of the breastfeeding, the running up and down stairs, and the constant activity. My arms were strong from carrying babies around and holding little children on my hip. It was an undertaking to get us all ready for church, but we still made it to every meeting with diaper bag, snacks, notebooks, and Bibles. It was also an undertaking to get all the kids to bed at night. It took an hour or two from the time baths were started, through the giving of drinks and the placing of kids back into bed, until everyone was finally asleep.

That fall we put two more boys into school at Laketon. Aaron went into the first grade with cousin Jeremy Bowers, and Joe started kindergarten with Chris. Andy moved up to second grade. The school pictures that year were priceless. In the foreground, there was a little boy in a plaid cowboy shirt smiling at the camera; in the background, the same little boy was in serious profile. The group picture of each class was just a rag-tag collection of country kids.

That was the last year of public school for us at Laketon. We decided to start home school as the boys went into first, second, and third grade. We were thinking they could get a better education that way. We hired a tutor named Cynthia to help us out.

Although these were hectic times, it helped to live where we did on the hill. The kids had yards and woods and fields to play in. They had sandboxes and bikes. Mom and Daddy were nearby to help with kids who overflowed to their house. They had their three cousins at the bottom of the hill. They had Uncle Mick and Aunt Jo Etta.

Living back off the road like we did, the kids were free to wear whatever clothes they wanted, and the little boys were free to go to the bathroom in the woods. They were free to run and yell. I was free to yell right back, "Get out of the mud! Leave Danny alone! Come inside!"

In the winter they sledded down the hill and up their snow ramp, flying through the air and landing with a bang. In the summer they flew down the lane on bikes. Just like I had done as a little girl, the kids used their imagination to pretend they were hunters, soldiers, Indians, athletes, cooks, or whatever else they wanted to be.

My dad planted a garden back in the field, adding more rows of vegetables each year until it filled both sides of the road. He and Jo Etta did most of the work, with some help from the kids, but I had all the fresh vegetables I wanted. Even with so many kids under my feet, I still found time to can tomatoes, green beans, pickles, and jelly. Daddy also planted a row of red raspberries behind his house. They grew tall and thrived because of all the garbage and melon rinds he dumped around them. I would walk down the row after meals and eat raspberries for dessert.

Whenever I could, I walked back to the garden or down the lane. On beautiful summer days I wanted to get outside with the kids. I imagined taking a walk with my happy children around me, getting some sun and enjoying nature. It hardly ever happened the way I imagined. Soon after leaving the house, there was usually arguing and crying. The same thing happened in the winter. I imagined kids playing together in the snow, all red cheeks and smiles. After an hour outfitting everyone with proper boots, hats, snowsuits, and mismatched gloves, I wondered if it was worth it. Finally they were out the door, but it wasn't long until someone was face down in the snow and back inside. Eventually they were all back in, peeling clothes off inside out, leaving wet muddy piles of boots and snowsuits for me to deal with. But it was worth it. They grew hale and hearty from being outside so much.

Our wooded hill was a great place for wildlife. We threw bread crumbs and birdseed on a picnic table in the winter and birds flocked in, blue jays and a dozen cardinals at a time, as well as woodpeckers and little nuthatches. We also had squirrels and chipmunks galore because of all the nut trees. Our house was set in a grove of walnut trees. In the fall, walnuts rolled down our roof like billiard balls and then the hulls turned black and rotted in our yard. Sometimes deer passed through the yard. Mom fed a stray cat, and before she knew it, she had fifteen cats trailing her in the yard. Snakes abounded. Sometimes a snake would slide into Jo Etta's house or the boys would carry a snake up to the house, stretched full length between them.

We got a golden retriever one winter while we lived in the house on the hill. He wasn't a mongrel like Nip—we had to pay for him. He was a tan, furry puppy when we brought him home, and because it was cold at the time, he had to stay in the house for a while. Jeff and the kids loved him. I said we should name him Skipper, and they all agreed. But I made him move outside as soon as he was big enough. "We're not having any dogs in the house," I said.

Daddy finished our garage and built an office into one corner for Jeff, so he was able to work at home and be nearby if I needed help with the kids. He studied in his office, then traveled to his weekly meetings. The longest trip was when he left Monday afternoon to go to the Zion Lake meeting and didn't return until after the Tuesday New Whiteland meeting, getting home after midnight.

Our whole family went to summer seminars at Zion Lake, a campground and meeting center in southern Indiana run by Don and Doris Langebartels. It was a beautiful, serene place. Don and Doris encouraged me to come to the seminars, saying there would be people there to help me out with the kids, but it was still hard. We were able to stay in the upstairs dorm, where there were lots of beds and plenty of room, but it got hot up there in the summer and bees flew in and out of the windows.

I would spend a day or two carefully packing for these trips, laying out little equivalent piles of clothing for each of the kids. One pair of pants, two pairs of shorts, four play shirts, two church shirts, underwear, and so on. I tried to think of everything we would need. Food was provided for us there, so I didn't have to worry about that. I liked talking to Don and Doris at Zion Lake, and I liked Sandi, their cook and helper. But I sometimes wondered why I even went to the seminars when I had to take care of crying babies during meetings or put the kids to bed while the adults were talking downstairs. After the first meeting and change of outfits, our big dorm room was a wreck of castoff clothing and diapers. But the good times outweighed the work.

At the end of 1984, Dr. Freeman died—of a sickness. We all said that Faith Assembly would go on. We all said that we didn't follow a man. But the church never recovered its days of glory. No one could take Dr. Freeman's place, and there were no plans about what to do because he hadn't expected to die at the age of sixty-four. Three of the ministers formed a co-leadership, and Jeff was also one of the recognized leaders in the church. The leaders tried to carry on, but the whole movement gradually declined as people began to sort out what they believed and many left to form their own groups or return to where they came from. It was an unsettling time, but we knew God's kingdom and the church didn't depend on any one person. It was something that had to happen for our own good.

BRYCE

By the time we were ready for our eighth baby to be born, we felt like we really knew what to expect in childbirth. We had our birthing stuff ready, and Mom and Jo Etta were lined up to babysit. Mick and Jo were taking Mom and Daddy on a vacation to see Elaine in South Dakota, but they would be back in plenty of time to help after the baby was born in the middle of June. On June 8, I woke up early in the morning and felt the familiar sensations of labor. As I lay in bed, I heard the van go down the lane on its way to South Dakota. This baby was coming a week early, but it wouldn't do to try to stop Mom and Daddy and ruin the only vacation they ever had besides that one trip to Kentucky.

Some friends who lived nearby came over to get the kids out of the house and Kelly, the midwife, arrived. While the kids were back in the field looking at cows, before we even figured out where they were going to go, Bryce Anthony was born at eight in the morning.

Kelly said, "Your babies just fall out."

That wasn't exactly true, but with Bryce it was close. If only they could have all been so fast and easy. We found other people in the church to help us out and called my family in South Dakota to tell them they had missed the baby's birth.

Bryce was another round-faced, healthy baby, between seven and eight pounds in weight. By this time I realized that if you put all my kids in the bathtub, got their hair wet, and slicked it back, their faces all looked alike.

We got the idea for Bryce's name from a little boy named Bryce who lived near our duplex in Warsaw. Bryce means "alert" and "quick-moving." Anthony means "priceless."

It had been just ten years since Andy was born. Besides our two girls, we had six boys now—three big and three little. We still refer to them that way. Andy, Aaron, and Joe liked to sit on the couch with their little brothers and read them library books by Bill Peet and Richard Scarry. Like all boys, they played with trucks and cars of every variety. I threw an old sheet over the table and drew roads and towns on it for all their little vehicles. They slowly ran their Matchbox cars along the edge of the table just so they could watch the wheels turn. In the sandbox, they dug holes and hills with all their construction equipment and tractors.

We had gotten a TV and VCR about this time so the kids could watch good videos like *National Geographic* programs that someone had recorded from TV. We played *Lions of Africa* over and over, fast-forwarding through the animal mating scenes. We let them watch documentaries from the library and movies like *Grizzly Adams*. I was very selective about what they could watch. We didn't want them to get in a habit of watching all the junk on TV, so we never turned it on. But they got a small dose of TV anyway because when they went up to Grandma and Grandpa's they watched *The Dukes of Hazzard* and *Little House on the Prairie*.

The kids became artists since they didn't watch TV all the time. They drew pictures and painted and colored. They were creative. They had to use their imaginations to think of things to do. They went outside and played. It wasn't a bad thing.

We gradually loosened up about movies over the years, but it was much later before we caught up with the times and watched *Star Wars, E.T., Jurassic Park,* and *Home Alone,* long after everyone else had seen them. The movie that finally got us back in the actual movie theater was *Gettysburg.*

Bryce's birth was easy, but the hard part came later. It wasn't because we added one more baby boy to our crowd. I was getting used to that. And it wasn't because the church was struggling after Dr. Freeman. It was what happened a year later.

Our second year of home school had just begun when Cynthia, the tutor, had an accident driving home one day. Another car hit her car from the side. Because she was so shaken up by the accident, she came back to spend the night with us instead of going on home. That one night with us turned into weeks and months. She had had a concussion in the accident so she got dizzy and fainted at times, but she felt she didn't have anywhere else to go because she and her husband were having marriage problems.

She had been an excellent teacher for the kids, loving them like her own, but I just didn't like having someone else in my home all the time, especially someone who was so dependent on me. I hardly left the house as I cared for her and my own family. A whole season of autumn colors passed me by.

Because our tutor couldn't continue teaching, we had to bring in another young lady as a tutor. Paula was a pretty young lady, very nice, but not used to country life. Two of our bedrooms were now taken up with these two women. I felt it wasn't my own home anymore.

But that wasn't the end of it. One morning I was called over to my parents' home to find my mom in bed, speaking in garbles, confused and unable to use one side of her body. Apparently she had had a stroke—my mom who had always prided herself in her health and strength. Daddy took good care of her as she began to recover. She tried her best to keep her dignity as she walked around the house in a nightgown, still having trouble talking. She couldn't write anything down, either. It always came out backwards and confused. I had thought she would make a complete recovery, but she kept having setbacks. She got so frustrated trying to talk to us. Sometimes when her words came out funny we laughed, until she got upset and we realized how much it hurt her.

By the middle of a muddy February, Cynthia was making a good recovery, and Mom was holding her own. We left all the kids with Cynthia and Paula to take a ski vacation at Keystone Resort in Colorado. I had learned to ski about a year before when I had been four months' pregnant, squeezing myself into navy ski pants under a light blue ski coat with matching hat and big pink mittens. I learned to ski on the easy slopes, falling in a gentle slide so neither bones nor baby would get hurt.

Keystone was beautiful in winter. I loved it. We took the ski lifts to the top of the mountain and looked out across the Rockies. Dark evergreens held up armloads of snow. Sometimes fresh flakes drifted down. It looked like a picture from a calendar. We skied down the mountain, slope after slope, vista after vista, until we got to the bottom. At noon we set our skis and poles against a rack and clunked over wooden walkways in ski boots to the lodge where hot soup and bread never tasted so good. One night we ate in a fancy restaurant in the resort, so fancy that the waiters placed the napkins in our laps and scooted crumbs off the table with little brushes. The food was in small portions but very expensive.

One night, and by this time I was chilled and feverish with a cold, we had Swiss fondue at the top of the mountain and then skied down the long easy slope at night. It was all such a nice break from reality but thoughts of my mom were always there in the background. We later found out the reason she wasn't getting better was because she had an inoperable tumor in her neck.

By April, Mom seemed to be getting worse. Daddy got her some roses on their anniversary, April tenth, but as roses often do, they died before they ever opened up. She seemed upset by it. Three weeks later, just after she had turned seventy, I was again called to their house in the morning. We had gotten home late the night before from the meeting in New Whiteland. I was congested and feeling terrible with a cold. Mom appeared to be in a coma. She looked so small in her bed, as helpless as a child. That evening she died at home with all her family around her. It was the first time I had ever seen death, but we knew Mom was in a new home in heaven.

Afterward, Daddy sat on the back porch between Mindy and me, his arms around us. He said, "It was how she would have wanted it. She didn't want to go on the way she was." We knew it was true, but it was still our mother who had died.

When the people from the funeral home came to take her body away, Daddy moved all the furniture and antiques away from the front door that they never used. He said, "She's not going out any back door."

She went out the right way, through the front door.

The next day I walked all over the fields on the property, giving in to tears, my nose red from crying and from my cold. I was thinking about my mother. She had lived so close to me and had helped so much with the kids, especially Renee and Vicki. They were devastated when she died. She was a second mom to them, adding an extra loving touch along with the Kool-aid and cookies.

I thought back of a trip that Mom and I had made to Fort Wayne a few years earlier. She had told me in detail, as one adult to another, what it had been like when Ralph had left her, how she had felt, and how it had affected Mick and Elaine. If only I could have recorded it, because now I didn't remember all those details. On that same trip I had turned a corner in the van and she slipped right off the captain's seat onto the floor because of her slippery skirt and the sharp turn. But she had just laughed. She didn't have a problem laughing at herself.

We had a very simple funeral, with just the immediate family, at the Laketon cemetery. I woke that morning thinking what a beautiful spring day, but for a funeral. Elaine and Riley had come from South Dakota. Elaine said that the best time to sort through a person's belongings was right after the funeral, when people were there to help and you were still numb with grief. As soon as we got home, she took us through the house, and we made decisions about everything. She was right. We didn't feel so much pain. When we sorted through the bathroom drawers, we found the little containers and perfume bottles Mom had never thrown away. She had been just like her own mom, saving things for no good reason.

For a long time afterward, whenever something interesting or special happened, my first thought was, *I'll call Mom and tell her.* Like I always had. Then I realized I couldn't, of course.

I used to get annoyed sometimes because Mom would call me every day. I would be in the middle of a helter-skelter day, and she would interrupt me with a call. She wouldn't start with a normal greeting, but would cheerily start in the middle of a thought, like, "The weatherman was right this time." Or, "So you're doing green beans today." She would talk about current events, and I would agree and agree, wanting to get off the phone. Now I would miss those calls.

Home, my original Mom-and-Dad home, would never be the same. It was now Daddy's home. He ran it much more simply. It was less cluttered, much more quiet, almost somber. He played old, scratchy records that they had bought when they joined the record club back at The Dutch Mill. I had grown up listening to *50 of the World's Greatest Music Treasures* and *25 Beloved Melodies,* classic haunting orchestra pieces that Daddy now started playing again. I think it reminded him of his life with Mom. He was lonely, but he could take care of himself and did fine.

Years before, Mom had planted a curving row of lilies on top of the hill. They came up in gushes of green leaves that soon wilted and died in the spring, about the same time Mom died. Then, in August, overnight, a single stem would shoot up from each plant, several inches tall with purple blooms on top. Mom had told me they were called Resurrection Lilies, because they died and then months later resurrected. Just like Mom will do someday.

By the end of the school year, Cynthia was well enough that she could move out on her own, so Paula could move out, too. I had to admit that because Cynthia and Paula had been living with us, I had been able to leave the house and help my mom at the end of her life. But now it was time for our family to look ahead. Jeff had been offered the job of leading Faith Assembly after Dr. Freeman's death, but he didn't want that responsibility. Nobody did. Jeff was also invited to move south to pastor a new church that would be formed by the merging of the New Whiteland group and two other groups around Indianapolis. As much as we didn't want to leave our home in the woods, we decided we couldn't pass up this opportunity. We decided to move to the Indianapolis area, and Mindy would move into our house.

RACHELLE

I discovered we were expecting another baby that summer. I had a lot of work to do, though, before we could move. We had lived in this house in the woods for six years, thinking we would stay there forever. We were firmly entrenched. I began sorting clothes into give-away and throw-away boxes. I started organizing our closets and packing things up. Then I tackled the garage with its cans of paint, old cassette tapes, and assorted parts from broken things. I wanted to leave the house nice for Mindy, so I scrubbed six-years'-worth of milk splashes off the kitchen wainscoting and used stain to touch up the woodwork.

We began looking for a country house to rent near Indianapolis that would be big enough for nine children. There were not many of those around. Somehow we heard of a big old country house near Greenfield. We called the owner, Ms. Snipes, but she said, "absolutely not" when she heard how many kids we had. She said the house was too nice, with its oriental rugs, chandeliers, and parquet floors. We told her our kids were well-behaved and we were responsible people and would she please at least meet with us so she could see how nice we were. She finally said okay.

We dressed nicely and drove down with our family to meet Ms. Snipes. She met us back with a hard stare. She never smiled as we presented our case and showed her flattering pictures of our present home so she could see how well we could take care of a house. She finally agreed to "give us a try," but she would charge a two-hundred-dollar security deposit each month, on top of the five-hundred-dollar rent. We would get the deposit back each year if the house passed her inspection.

We packed all our possessions onto a flatbed semi-truck and moved to Greenfield with our eight kids—and Skipper. I was five months' pregnant at the time. We said a tearful goodbye to Daddy, Mindy, Mick, Jo, and the kids, gave one last glance at our house, and then drove down the lane.

The people from the new church were eager to help. Mr. Hunt, who lived nearby, provided the semi-truck and helped us move. When we got to the house, loads of people were there to help us move in. They had set up tables full of food on the front porch where I was to sit and direct traffic while they did all the work. The women in the church had already painted many of the rooms and scrubbed the windows and cupboards, as well as had new carpet installed. We felt very loved and welcome. The big white house had rooms galore, including five bedrooms, two living rooms, an attic, and a full basement. A garage, several outbuildings, a big, red barn, and yards the size of football fields surrounded the house.

With so many rooms and doors, our new house swallowed us up that first night. I tried to find logical places to organize clothes and shoes as we rounded the kids up for bed. I was very tired but happy about our new adventure, thankful we had been able to get this beautiful old house, thankful for our new southern friends.

Jeff was excited about his new position as pastor, uniting the church groups from New Whiteland, Greenfield, and Indianapolis. The people worked together like a family to build the new church. They had good intentions for the new building, but it ended up looking like a military bunker surrounded by earth ramparts. The landscaping never took hold, so it always looked scrappy—not like a church at all. But the two to three hundred people that made up Faith Christian Assembly were zealous, and they loved us.

Rachelle was born on January 28, during the middle of our first winter in the big white house. A midwife from the new church was there to help out, and that's all I remember about the experience. Childbirth was becoming an almost routine event. Like the three boys before, Rachelle weighed between seven and eight pounds. We hardly bothered to weigh the babies anymore—just knowing that they were about seven pounds was good enough. We named our little girl Rachelle, a form of Rachel meaning "lamb," and Eileen, meaning "shining light," in honor of my mother. She had light brown hair and the familiar round face with big cheeks.

No matter how many children we had, each birth was still a miracle. Each baby was a wonder, a normal, healthy little person. Partly me, partly Jeff, but one-of-a-kind, as we soon found out each time as they grew older.

When Rachelle was two months old, she went on two major trips with us: an all-out family vacation to Gulf Shores, Alabama, and a ministry trip to England. Both trips were taken with our friends Fred and Susie.

We drove to Alabama with all nine kids and a babysitter, distributed between our van and Fred and Susie's Cadillac. As soon as we made it to Gulf Shores and had carried all of our gear up the steps to the condominium, we let the kids loose. It was a bright, sunny day, and the kids romped on the beach. They stayed out for hours as we settled in and fixed supper. No one thought about suntan lotion. No one had suspected that the sun was that hot, but the next morning the kids were all in pain. All of them were sunburned, slightly swollen and feverish. Our first full day there, they had to lie around and play inside. But there was still plenty of time for fun. The boys visited the *U.S.S. Alabama*, and all the kids made sand castles, chased sea gulls, and jumped in the waves, while Baby Rachelle slept soundly in the condominium most of the time.

But all fun things must come to an end. We had to drive all the way back home. As we reached Elizabethtown, Kentucky, fire shot out the back of the van as an axle broke, and we had to stop. We had the van towed to a nearby garage where they said they would have to order parts in order to fix it. There was nothing else to do but sit and wait. At least there was a Royal Inn motel and a truck stop nearby. Nine kids, four adults, and a teenager piled into two or three rooms to wait it out. It took three days. Every morning we would go to the truck stop and have a Kentucky breakfast of eggs, sausage, grits, and pancakes, and then all fourteen of us would sit in the parking lot of the Royal Inn. We sat on the steps while the kids walked around the edge of the parking lot on the cement edging or tossed a football around. At lunch and suppertime, we walked back over to the truck stop to eat, and then returned to sit in the parking lot or our rooms.

The Royal Inn was run by immigrants from India who had incense smoldering and oriental idols sitting in the lobby. It was too creepy to spend much time in there. Finally, after three days, the parts came in, the van was fixed, and we were on our way.

Not long after this trip, we took Rachelle with us to England with Fred and Susie. England lived up to its reputation of being rainy, gloomy, and chilly. We toured London with our English friends, pushing Baby Rachelle down the sidewalk in a fancy British pram. I remember nursing Rachelle under my raincoat while walking down a London street crowded with people. I loved the countryside and the small towns the best. Driving down a curvy, wooded lane on the left side of the road, I felt like I was in a Sherlock Holmes novel.

We visited a family in their narrow home, one room wide, part of a long row of houses bristling with chimneys. After passing through the hedge and tiny front yard, we entered the living room. Beyond it was the dining room; beyond that was the kitchen. As I looked out the kitchen window at the old brick buildings with slate roofs and black chimneys against cloudy gray skies, I felt like it was 1942, and I would not have been surprised to hear warplanes drone overhead.

We returned home to a dry summer—the drought of 1988. The grass turned brown, so crisp and prickly it hurt your feet to walk on it barefoot. The corn was stunted in the fields. That summer, the Dukes family from Texas came to visit us, and I remember discussing with them the book, *88 Reasons Why Jesus Will Return in 1988*. We all agreed that it was foolish to make that prediction, and of course, Jesus didn't return in 1988.

The kids loved living in the big white house surrounded by corn and soybean fields near Greenfield. It was a place for adventures. The kids spent hours playing in the big red barn across the road and making forts in the hay. The boys climbed on the barn rafters and swung like monkeys from the big tree in the back yard. One spring we found an astonishing six-hundred mushrooms in the woods. The boys explored the woods and streams with Skipper bounding along to keep them company.

The adventures never stopped. Danny, Scott, and Bryce were just the right age for building forts and trails. It was too bad they didn't realize that it was poison-ivy vines they were yanking out to make their trail! They ended up in bed with poison ivy from head to toe. When an entire apple tree—including the treehouse with Scott and Bryce in it—crashed down, I was thankful they didn't break their necks. Then Scott ran his hand through the glass front door instead of opening it properly, and he still has a v-shaped scar to show for it.

But for as many kids as we had, and all the dangers there were in the country, we didn't have that many mishaps over the years. Danny fell on a stiff thorn and broke it off in his hand. We had thought we had gotten it all out, but a few weeks later, it worked its way through and came out the other side. But no problem. Vicki bit through her tongue while sledding. Renee accidentally ran the sewing-machine needle through her finger. Everyone has a little scar on their forehead or near their eyebrow where they fell against a coffee table or the corner of a wall. Rachelle fell through ice on the pond, but Andy rescued her. Kids slipped underwater, but someone always pulled them out. Kids got lost in stores or at the zoo, but we always found them. Someone got lost in a cornfield but found their way out. We did the best we could, and God was always watching over them, too.

The big white house in the country was a place for sports. The boys played endless basketball games at their little full court made of two portable goals set up inside the barn or at the dirt half-court sloping away from the hoop nailed to the side of the barn. The girls tried out gymnastics on the front-yard grass. The yards were perfect for baseball or football. Inside the house, the kids tumbled and did flips on the old king-sized mattress we put on the extra living-room floor. We left it there for months. The stairs were good for sliding down on slippery nylon sleeping bags.

Everyone learned to work when we lived there. The boys mowed those huge yards with a push mower, six boys taking turns until it was done. They earned a few coins helping Ms. Snipes pick up stones out of her fields, and the older boys helped a pig farmer down the road. They baled hay and caught squealy pigs for him, but the hardest part was getting him to pay them later.

Corn de-tasseling was one of the boys' first official jobs, although you wouldn't have heard of such a thing unless you lived in a "corn state" like Indiana. For about three weeks, the older boys joined a gang of kids in the early morning dew to walk up and down long corn rows like little slaves, pulling off the tassels so the fields would produce seed corn. But the boys came to love the feeling of earning their own money.

When Andy got his driver's license, we gave him the long, yellow Cadillac that Fred and Susie had given us when they were done with it, and he began working at Burger King in Greenfield. He soon switched to McDonalds and started a family tradition for us. The next five kids in a row worked at McDonalds until it became a joke with them: "Here comes another Barney to work at McDonalds." Not that they weren't happy to get our kids. They were all good workers.

I tried to get all the work I could out of the kids at home. I read the book, *365 Ways to Get Your Kids to Help at Home*. It was loaded with ideas for job charts, it had lists of what chores were best for different age groups, and it said that the golden age for kids to help at home was between six and twelve. I had several in that age bracket. I experimented with the ideas in the book, but the most helpful was a cardboard chart with pockets for rotating job lists. I had age-appropriate jobs for everyone, and although it never worked perfectly, and I wasn't a very good taskmaster, it did help.

I actually ended up doing most of the work myself. Just cooking for our family was a huge job. Because all the kids were at home all day, we sat around our ten-foot table for lunch and supper. We usually alternated between a chicken dish and a hamburger dish. I spent a lot of time preparing meals in tall pots and long casserole dishes, which were then placed in the center of the table. We all gathered around, Jeff prayed, portions were dished out, and we dug in. I took pride in knowing that I had fixed something good for my family.

The food was gone in a few minutes, it seemed, then leaving a family-sized mess to clean up. There was the high chair, table, floor, kitchen counters, and stove, all needing work. The kids did help somewhat, according to the job chart, and it felt good to get everything clean and back in its place. I finished by wiping off all the counters and sweeping the floor. Everything looked nice again. It was one job where I could see immediate results, not like other parts of being a mom, like discipline or teaching values, where you never know how well you're doing until years later when the kids are grown up.

With a family this size, discipline was an issue. You couldn't use psychology every time you wanted something done, or think of creative ways every day to reward good behavior and discourage bad behavior. We had to use the paddle. The Bible said that if we loved our kids, we would spank them when they needed it. It was the only way. Of course, I read books about discipline, but it was hard to be consistent and fair in the actual practice of it. A friend who was a woodworker gave us a dozen unfinished flat wooden spoons, so they became paddles that were handy anywhere around the house—until the kids hid them or threw them away. I tried to keep one or two on top of the refrigerator. It became a longstanding joke that I was always feeling around on top of the refrigerator for a paddle. As the boys got older, I had trouble spanking them. They would run away or twist around as I held them by one arm. They laughed that they were getting too big for me. I said, "I'll just have to tell Dad when he gets home."

One of the hardest things to deal with was the rivalry and fighting between the kids themselves. Aaron and Joe would gang up against Andy. Renee and Aaron didn't get along. Danny and Scott would fight. As the youngest boy, Bryce was always picked on. Renee and Vicki picked on whoever was younger than them. Most of the time, I would try to separate the kids just to make peace.

We lived in the white house during the 1980s in all its fashion glory. I had never been very good about taking care of my little girls' hair, choosing to just let it fall where it would, but now I had preteen girls. They worked on each other's hair, pulling it to the side in pony tails, piling it up in stiff waves above their foreheads, as was the style. Neon colors were in, as well as wearing different patterns together with thick socks in all colors. I went into a sewing frenzy. Now that I had girls to sew for and someone had given me a sewing machine, I started making sundresses in hot pink and lime green, culottes, nightgowns, and fancy dresses with lace collars. I could hardly wait to start a new project. But after nineteen items, I got tired of it and stopped. The same happened with counted cross stitch. I loved it for a while, I completed several projects as a creative way to relax, and then I was done with it.

We didn't go out to eat much as a family, except to Pizza Hut. Anywhere else would have been too expensive. Only a few brave people ever asked us into their homes for supper, like our good friends Jim and Donna Marchand. They weren't afraid to feed all of us and even have us stay overnight in their home. Besides eating, we would play games like Balderdash and have basketball tournaments—Jeff and our boys against Jim and his two boys. Mr. Marchand could always make us laugh. Donna would fix us a whole counter full of food. Jim said, "It's like having a plague of locusts come through. All of our food is gone when you leave."

But for such a large family, we did go places.

Andy said, "Who's gonna care that we went to Sea World?"

Well, we did go to Sea World and to Cedar Point amusement park on the same trip with the eight oldest kids. It was over two hundred dollars each time—just to get us in the doors—plus we had to pay for two or three hotel rooms each night. I imagine that we just put it on the credit card and dealt with it later.

Jeff and the kids loved the roller coasters, but I didn't get a "thrill" out of "thrill rides." Besides, someone had to stay with little Bryce, who wasn't tall enough to ride the big rides. Bryce and I went on the log run and the bumper cars.

My favorite trips were to the zoo or to Conner Prairie in Indianapolis, where the kids could see living history. All the people at the Prairie had to stay in character, as if it were the 1800s. It was very educational, just like it was at the Fort Wayne Fort. The people there would talk about wars and Indians as if they were just outside of town.

You could ask the women who were cooking, "Aren't you hot cooking over that fire? Don't you hate all those flies?"

They said, "Yes, but there's nothing we can do about it, is there?" There wasn't anything they could have done about it back then.

I liked seeing how people used to live. I thought about the immigrants, like the Gearharts and McQuistons, who had come to America for a better life, crossing the ocean by boat and maybe even seeing the Statue of Liberty when they arrived. I thought about the pioneers who had moved west with their families, including little kids, looking for a better home. Those were the bravest people.

The kids were reading the *Little House on the Prairie* books, so I read them, too, by dim light at nap time. I liked *The Long Winter* the best, with all those blizzards, snow covering up their house, snow coming in through the cracks, and the Ingalls were down to just baked potatoes to eat. It made baked potatoes sound so good that I fixed them for supper.

One summer we tried camping at Clifty Falls in southern Indiana. We had three tents—one for us, one for the boys, and one for the girls. We cooked hot dogs over the open fire and ate potato chips and Oreos. We told stories and took hikes down the trails. The six boys took off on a hike by themselves and returned much later, one by one. We found out that they had gone on the most strenuous six-mile trail down the rocky creek bed. We asked the little boys how they had made it. They said that the big boys had told them if they didn't keep up, they'd just get left behind.

We had so much fun there that we went to the little convenience store and bought some more hot dogs and supplies in order to stay another night. We swam at the pool, hiked, and cooked over the fire. We were all still having so much fun that we bought even more supplies and stayed a third night. Then we went home.

AUDREY

One more baby was born in the big white house, our tenth, and she was the only one born in the fall. Once again, everything was ready, and I went into labor. I took a walk down the road and around the graveyard, hoping to speed things up. Audrey Christine was born in the evening of October 23, 1989. Audrey means "noble strength," and Christine means "Christian." She weighed about seven pounds, and she had light hair—everything was normal. All of the kids stayed with friends for a while so that I could rest, and then it was back to our usual house full of action. As a baby, Audrey reached up and played with my earlobes when I held her. I had trouble keeping on my earrings during church.

Not long after Audrey was born, Jeff said that God told him clearly as I walked around the bed one morning that I was through having babies. I wasn't sure that I could believe him, because of past experience and because I was only thirty-eight, but it turned out that he was right.

We had a perfect ten—three boys and two girls, then three boys and two girls. It was almost as if it had been planned that way. Actually, we believe that it had been planned that way by God Himself.

I sat down one day and did the math. From the first to the last birth fourteen years had passed. Altogether I had been pregnant for a full seven-and-a-half years. I had been pregnant more months than I had not been, and even then, I had been breastfeeding. Six babies were born in the summer.

Maternity clothes were important to me, and I thought they should be comfortable. I wore lots of denim jumpers and flowing tent-like dresses toward the end of the nine months. For six summers, I spent my time barefoot in sundresses, drinking iced tea. I still won't wear denim jumpers or anything that resembles a maternity outfit to this day.

We continued to home school the children. Cynthia, our tutor, had moved down with us and lived nearby. The kids were getting a good education and learning to read well. I have to give

Cynthia credit for the job she did, but it was expensive, and I finally decided that we should switch to Abeka video school. It was hard to break this news to Cynthia, who loved our family, but it was a change I wanted to make.

We bought two more TVs and two VCRs and then ordered the books and tapes. The curriculum was advanced compared to that of the public school, as well as being more conservative and wholesome. I loved looking at the new books and smelling their fresh smell. The kids listened to their classes on tape, almost as if they were part of a classroom, and then they did their homework. I monitored the school and helped the ones who were learning to read, which, by this time, were Danny, Scotty, and Bryce. It was a great idea in theory, but sometimes the kids didn't watch all the tapes or pay attention. I had a hard time teaching the kids to read. We had to record their reading so that the people at Abeka could evaluate how we were doing. As we played the tapes back, I could hear myself prompting them in the background, practically putting the words in their mouths as they struggled to read. It was both painful and funny at the same time.

I helped the older kids with projects on Indiana history and tried to make sure they watched the videos and did their work. When we were done with a box of videos, I had to box them up and ship them back. School was quite a task.

Sometimes the weather itself was an adventure. While growing up, I had listened to the weatherman, Earl Finkle, on WOWO, as he described the winter storms forming in the Texas panhandle then coming up the Ohio valley to Indiana. I had always wanted to be right in the heaviest snow band. I loved storms and changing weather. I never went outside without looking up at the sky, at the daytime clouds or the sunset, just as at night I always looked up at the stars. I called the kids out to watch the summer storms and lightning. I commented on snow, rainbows, humidity, and sunsets to whoever would listen.

We were living in the big white house during the famous spring ice storm, when the ice coated everything in an inch-thick layer, from electric lines and fences down to every blade of grass.

When the sun came out the next day and glittered on the trees, they looked like crystal figurines. Jeff took pictures of icy fences and mailboxes that were so beautiful we should have sent them in to *Country* magazine. (We'd been in *Country* magazine before. Renee had sent in our family picture, writing that we took walks at dusk and the boys played basketball by the barn. We showed up in *Country Extra* right next to some big Amish families.)

Despite its beauty, the ice storm was destructive. Branches of trees snapped off, leaving white points sticking out in all directions, almost as if a tornado had gone through. A whole row of tall steel electric towers came down like dominoes, so we were without electricity for days.

After half a day in the cold house with no water we knew we had to leave. Fred and Susie told us to come down to their place because they had electricity at their home. As we climbed into the van with our kids and bags of clothes, the ice crackling in the wind, the yard littered with branch debris, I felt like we were refugees leaving a war-torn land. At least we had a nice warm place to go, with people who loved our kids and would feed us good southern food.

Fred and Susie took care of us until we could go back home. That's the way these church people were, always there for us. And it wasn't just Fred and Susie. Marjorie had helped us with all of our decorating, making curtains for the house in the woods and also for this house. She made navy-blue bedspreads for three of the boys. She made pillows; she painted; she cleaned windows; she helped pick out wallpaper. She turned the milk house into a study for Jeff, using designer ideas like covering the walls with fabric and sticking pieces of straw into the ceiling paint. Her husband had worked at all kinds of different occupations, and he seemed to know something about everything, so he was there if we ever needed advice.

There was also another young couple who was willing to watch all of our kids if we ever needed to go somewhere. I was able to travel with Jeff when he spoke in different parts of the country and even went back to Germany again. They took in the kids like they were their own.

Another lady in the church came every week to clean our house and watch the kids so that I could do my weekly shopping. I spent an hour at the library picking out books and acceptable videos for the kids before I went to the grocery store. Even after I came home and we had lunch, this lady stayed long enough for me to take a nap. I used to study during nap time, but now with ten kids, I went to sleep even if it took me an hour to shake off the grogginess when I woke up. That was how I made it through the rest of the day.

These were great people who loved us and helped us. But some of them were the very ones who opposed us when we tried to bring change to the church. We heard of exciting things happening in the rest of the charismatic movement, and we wanted to be a part of it. We were beginning to realize that we had isolated ourselves from the rest of the Christian world, almost as if we were trapped inside our church, in a room without a view. Jeff tried to get people to listen to different teachers and ideas, but he was yanked back and forth by factions in the church until he was in despair.

Some of these close friends would quote Jeff's own tapes, or Dr. Freeman's tapes, trying to prove his new ideas were wrong.

"You said this on your tape..."

"Dr. Freeman said..."

Jeff couldn't seem to hold the church together. When he followed his heart and became excited about the new things God was doing, these leaders of the church would accuse him of leaving the truth. When he leaned back toward them to save the church, he lost the people who wanted to move on. He ended up losing people on both sides. It was a dark time of depression for him. He became quiet and withdrawn. He questioned his leadership and looked for a way out, even thinking that maybe he should leave the ministry and do something else like go back to school and become a counselor.

We took long walks down country roads and talked. Jeff loved the smell of the growing corn in the summer, the smell of dry beans and cornstalks at harvest time. I liked it, too. I said that I always wanted to live in a place where I could walk down a country road or back into the woods. Most of our walks led us to the graveyard not far from our house, where we discussed church and people and God and eternity. We read the names on the gravestones, and eternity seemed nearby.

But we had other issues to deal with, too. We had gradually won over Ms. Snipes until she seemed satisfied with us as renters. She liked our kids because they were industrious, but we still had the house inspection each year. I tried to make the boys be careful with the soft walls in their bedrooms and the wall down the stairs, but it was an old house and the plaster was crumbly. They couldn't seem to keep from banging into the walls and making dents, which eventually turned into holes. I repaired the holes the best I could with joint compound and covered the spots with posters. Their bedroom was full of posters, but Ms. Snipes was smart. She knew about the walls.

At first she said it wasn't a big problem, because it wouldn't cost much to repair. But then the boys accidentally broke some glass shades on several of her valuable light fixtures. And the walls kept getting worse. Finally Ms. Snipes told us that we needed to move. We didn't get our deposit back for the first time in six years.

We started looking for another big house to rent in the country, which was not an easy thing to do. But we did find one.

We drove to the other side of Greenfield to check out the house I had seen advertised in the paper. When we turned down a gravel road, we saw a red brick ranch-style house, very simple, but surrounded by full grown trees like a woods. Behind the house, the yard sloped down to a little pond, with woods beyond that. I thought it was beautiful. It reminded me of our home up north in the woods.

As we walked around to the wooden deck in the back, a flock of geese flew in, their wings outstretched, and landed on the pond, right on cue. It was just like a picture on a wildlife calendar, and was almost like a sign to us that we should live here.

But then we walked inside and I realized right away that it was too small. It only had three small bedrooms and was only 1,600 square feet, including the garage. It was cute, with a wood stove, a nice kitchen, and a beautiful view, but cute isn't big enough for twelve people. We talked to the landlord who lived in the house next door. His name was Clyde, from Kentucky, from a big family like ours. He understood us and liked us. I said that though the house was too small, everything else seemed perfect. We had to find something soon, and we wished there was some way it could work.

I went home and made a drawing of the house on grid paper using the actual dimensions. Then I made little cutouts of our beds and furniture, all to scale, just to see if we could possibly fit in that space. After much rearranging, I finally decided that we could, and we called back and said we would take the house.

Again we had to sort and pack our possessions after six years of living in one place. Again we had become entrenched, this time filling up even more space, from the attic to the basement. But now we had to scale way back. We had our first garage sale to get rid of the extra stuff.

It was sad to leave the big white house, but we were always ready for something new. We drove away, looking at the front yard where the kids had once lined up in two rows with Skipper smiling at one end like he was part of the family. It had been a wonderful place to live. But Skipper didn't move with us because he had died.

There was only one way to arrange the furniture in our new house—the way I had figured it out on paper. There was no place for our ten-foot table. For the first time, we had to split up when we ate. The little dining area held our oval antique table with room for five or six of us, but the rest had to sit on stools at the bar counter. By now the older kids weren't always home at mealtime, so it worked out.

Four boys had to move into a nine-by-ten bedroom. Bunk beds stood on each side of the room, leaving a two-foot aisle down the middle. It looked like a bunkroom in a submarine. The older boys took charge of organization. Each boy got one fourth of the closet space and one fourth of the space under the beds for their clothes and such things as baseball cards.

Four girls went into another bedroom, Jeff and I had a bedroom, and that left two little boys to sleep on the floor in the living room. It would be like camping out every night. Each morning the little boys rolled up their sleeping bags into the corner. It worked out fine. Who says that everybody has to have his own room with a bedspread and a dresser?

In one corner of the garage, we built a little room for Jeff's office, but he soon moved into an office at the church, and that meant we had another bedroom. Like musical chairs, everyone rearranged themselves, and the little boys advanced from the floor to the bunk beds. As the older boys graduated from school and moved on, more bedroom space opened up. Eventually the big girls were put in the garage room, the little girls had a room, and the three little boys had a room. These bedrooms were just a hodge-podge of colors and materials, with no matching bedspreads and curtains or matching dressers and nightstands. Sleeping bags were the usual bed coverings, except for those three navy-blue bedspreads that Marjorie had made, which will probably last forever.

It turned out that Clyde was a good landlord and a good neighbor. At first I was a little nervous about him. He was a Vietnam veteran, with scars to show for it, and he had a large collection of guns in his house. Sometimes he held target practice in his back yard, right next to ours. Of course, Jeff and the boys were fascinated by the guns, but it turned out all right. Clyde and the boys just shot guns together from his back porch.

PART 3

A life is like a recipe box full of cards, jammed full of ordinary days and a few extraordinary ones—like a shoebox full of pictures that need to be sorted out.
I can't bring out all the cards in the box. I can't recount a lifetime of happenings. But I can tell you about a few extraordinary days, and I can sort the pictures into piles, one for each child.

CHAPTER 10

ANDY

"Mom, it's great if you write a book, but you gotta tell about Russia."

I've got to tell about Russia because Andy spent a year and a half of his life there. Going to Russia helped us turn a spiritual corner and make a break with the past.

Rusty Tardo from New Orleans visited our church and told us, "Y'all need to get out. *Go on a mission trip to Russia like our church did. Work with some other Christians. See what's going on in the world.*"

Rusty pastored a church much like ours. We agreed with him when he said of our movement, "*We don't have friends; we just have doctrines.*"

Jeff and I wanted to change, and we wanted to bring the church along with us.

Two amazing trips to Russia followed, in which we worked side by side with Christians from other churches, Christians from different backgrounds. It was a healthy experience for us. I went on the second trip, landing in Moscow and traveling to the city of Saratov by the Volga River. I saw so many things. The endless countryside rolling by from a Russian train. Wooden houses with bright trim and little gardens. Red Square. Slim pretty girls with skirts and blouses. Hopeful young men wearing American blue jeans. Buildings in disrepair. Tired old people with Soviet military badges on their chests.

I also saw Russian people filling the circus arena to hear about God and how to find salvation in Jesus. They listened and responded and were happy to receive the Bibles we handed out.

But I want to talk about Andy. We had put the older boys back in public school when they were in sixth and seventh grade. Each year we kept enrolling more and more children, in lower and lower grades, until Audrey started public school in first grade. Home school had gotten too frustrating for me, and the kids needed something more.

Now that Andy was about to graduate from Eastern Hancock High School, I laid a list of college majors in front of him.

"Do any of these sound interesting to you, Andy?" I asked.

"I don't know. I don't think so," he answered.

Andy's first love was clearly music. As a little boy, he had picked up anything lying around and played it like a guitar. As he grew older, his passion became the drums. He not only played the drums in our church, but at any odd moment, you might see him playing invisible drums in the air. He would imitate percussion sounds or sing songs with gusto. He also had a heart for God. Because he had no definite plans after graduation, he volunteered to go to Russia in 1995 as part of a team planting a new church in Saratov.

We stuffed a huge army duffel bag with everything Andy would need for the trip. For the Russian winters, we packed a warm mountain parka and thick lined boots from L.L. Bean. We jammed in clothes, long underwear, sturdy plastic kitchenware, a cookbook, and the *Zion Chronicles* historical novels for him to read on lonely nights. With his guitar and his bag, he was ready to go, but it was a strange feeling to send my firstborn son away, not to a nearby college, but to Russia—which not so long ago had been the Soviet Union, the home of the KGB and Stalin.

Andy wrote us letters from Russia and kept a diary. He had his own method of remembering Russian names by referring to soundman Eugene, white hair Eugene, drummer Dima, curly hair Dima, turtleneck Sergei, and so forth. And there was Igor, Natasha, Oxsana, and Alex, always an Alex.

Andy said that every morning the team prayed that God would give them "normal" people and families for the church. He said we wouldn't believe some of the things that go on there, things that were considered normal to Russians. The Americans would shake their heads and say, "They're crazy."

Life in Russia was tedious—searching the markets for eggs, trying to get the Russians together on time, getting from place to place by buses and trolleys. Andy said that he knew he was living in Russia when he got his outrageous fox hat. He saw real Russian ballet, but he was more excited when he got to practice with the Saratov basketball team and show them some American basketball skills. He said he did all right.

When I wrote to Andy, I always asked if he was eating well. If he was left to himself, he ate tuna, sausage, soup packets, and sugar donuts, or he would invent dishes by just tossing things together. But sometimes he had supper with the folks from Louisiana and then he had real Cajun food like jambalaya.

Andy was part of the praise and worship team, but he also did some preaching in small home groups and was there to help wherever he was needed in the business of planting a new church in a foreign country. His diary entries usually ended with "Read my daily Bible reading, did pushups, went to bed."

Whether it was the best thing or not, whether we should have insisted Andy go to college or not, he still had the adventure of a lifetime. How many people can say they spent a year and a half in Russia?

While Andy was there, my dad went to the doctor because he felt so tired and he had a pain in his side. The doctors said that he had a form of leukemia, but it wasn't the most serious kind. They said he would die of something else before he died of leukemia.

Daddy was seventy-five and beginning to look smaller, more frail. It was uncomfortable to see this because he had always been so strong. Just a few years before, he had rebuilt his house after a fire that had started behind the woodstove and spread through the roof. It had looked hopeless as we waded through wet debris on the floors and looked up through holes in the roof. Many antiques and collectibles were gone, but Daddy cleaned it all up. He had the remaining antiques cleaned of smoke damage, he rebuilt the roof with grandson Bryan's help, and he had new wallpaper put up. The new house was cleaner and more streamlined than ever. But that was his last big effort.

AARON

> *"This nephrotic syndrome is most likely caused by Minimal Change Disease. Eighty percent of the time that is what causes nephrotic syndrome in young adults, and it should respond to prednisone," Dr. Chong said. "We'll try that first before we do a biopsy."*

It was 1994. Andy was about to graduate from high school, and Aaron and Joe were juniors. We had taken Aaron to Dr. Swinney in Indianapolis, who sent us on to Dr. Chong, the nephrologist. But the huge dose of Prednisone didn't help, and the biopsy showed a much more serious kidney disease, *membranous proliferative glomerulonephritis*.

"So, now what?" we asked Dr. Chong.

"We can treat the high blood pressure, but it will most likely progress to kidney failure. The options then are dialysis and a kidney transplant."

Dr. Swinney told us, "Don't think you could have done anything to prevent this disease. We don't know what causes it, maybe a virus or something. But we don't know."

Aaron was only seventeen. It broke my heart. During his school physicals, they had said his blood pressure was a little high. We had also noticed some swelling in his legs. We had always believed that God could heal anything, but we were beginning to realize that the subject of healing was more complicated than we had thought. We were ready to do whatever was necessary for Aaron.

I had struggled for years with what Dr. Freeman had taught about divine healing. It wasn't that I doubted God would heal, but I questioned the way medical science was put down and discouraged. I was always trying to build up my faith, looking at it from every angle, reading books, and asking God about it. I would stare out the window wondering where all this would lead.

Now we were faced with the hardest test of all. The disease did progress to kidney failure, and Aaron did eventually go on peritoneal dialysis. But Aaron's life story is not about his disease. His story is about disregarding and overcoming disease, about not letting it keep him from what he wanted to do. Even when dialysis took up hours of his time every day, he still took a full course load at school and worked on the side.

On our many trips to Indianapolis to see the doctor, Aaron would tell me. "I always want to be the best at everything I do. I like to work hard and accomplish things. I hate quitting."

And that's the way Aaron has always been. He started working early, picking up stones out of the fields for Ms. Snipes and de-tasseling corn. Later, he worked in a little country grocery store and at McDonalds, where he was a junior manager. He always did more than was required, and his employers loved him.

Aaron said, "Grandpa Gearhart told me to always do a little more than your boss tells you to do, and you'll succeed at any job."

He set fitness goals for himself, keeping track of his running and lifting routines. He even made his brother Joe work out with him, helping Joe to lose weight and get in shape. Aaron stayed up late after church to finish his homework instead of putting it off. When we encouraged him to read the Bible, he set up a schedule for himself and read it straight through.

Aaron graduated third in his class and received several scholarships and awards, including the Alumni Scholarship that paid his entire tuition to Indiana State University at Terre Haute. He had chosen Indiana State because of their good aerospace program, and he went right ahead with his plans. He had always dreamed of being an airplane pilot, and so he began taking flight lessons and took various jobs working at airports.

Aaron loved the freedom of living on his own at school after having had to share everything at home. That fall he joined the Pi Kappa Alpha fraternity and tried out for their trike team, not reporting his kidney condition on the medical form. The trike race was a big event at Indiana State. They practiced hard for this relay race on oversized tricycles. His fraternity, known as the Pikes, had a tradition of winning, and Aaron made the team. We cheered Aaron on. The Pike team, dressed in tight yellow racing suits, won again. If Aaron was determined to do something, he did it.

After a year on dialysis, we began to prepare for the kidney transplant. With our big family, we figured that someone would be a match. Jeff and I took our four oldest kids to the IU Medical Center in Indianapolis to give blood for testing. We walked down the hospital hallways like a small group on a field trip, joking with each other in order to keep our spirits up. Several weeks later, we received six letters in the mail, one for each person who had been tested. It turned out that Jeff was the closest match, although Andy and Renee could also be donors. Joe was disappointed that he had a different blood type and couldn't be the donor for his brother since they were such close friends. I had a different blood type, too.

The transplant was a success, even though Aaron had an acute rejection during the first week. He started his senior year of college just a month later. He had to make many trips back to the hospital to solve various problems over the next few months, but things leveled out and Aaron was feeling good again. Aaron took some flight lessons but decided not to become a pilot. Flight school was expensive, and it would have been hard to get a commercial license with the kidney transplant. He finished college right on schedule with a degree in airport administration. He got a job with a new airline in Las Vegas and decided to move there.

JOSEPH

Don Langebartels came back from feeding the cows at Zion Lake with our three little boys. "You know, Joe is really smart," he said.
"Really, why?"
"I can just tell by the questions he asks."

Don was right. I hadn't noticed it myself because I was so caught up with taking care of my growing family of six or seven at the time. Joe was in kindergarten and had just learned the alphabet. I began to pay closer attention. Joe would sit at the kitchen table with library books, spelling out words to me and asking what they were.

"What is *c-h-a-i-r*?" he asked.

"That would be chair," I said.

Joe taught himself how to read. The following year when we started home school, Joe zipped through the first-grade books by the end of the first semester.

Cynthia, the tutor, said, "Joe's not being challenged. I think you should let him jump up to second grade with Aaron."

So that's what we did. Although Aaron was a hard act to follow, Joe joined him for second grade, and they stayed together like twins until graduation. They were the best of friends.

Joe was mischievous as a little boy, picking on his younger brothers, using his brain to talk his way out of trouble, but as a teenager, he showed the strength of his character after he wrecked Aaron's Camaro. Aaron had reluctantly let him borrow his white Camaro thinking, *What could happen? He's just going a few blocks in town.*

It turned out that a lot could happen. Joe ran into a telephone pole while he was adjusting the radio, wrecking the white Camaro that Aaron had so carefully cleaned and fixed up to sell for three thousand dollars. It was too bad about the car, but Joe was fine. He faithfully paid Aaron back the entire amount, a little at a time.

Joe was the valedictorian of his graduating class, but Aaron was close behind, coming in third. They both received awards and scholarships. Both were awarded the local Brooks scholarship, receiving several thousand dollars each.

We had a graduation party on our deck after the commencement ceremony, just like we had done for Andy and would do for all the kids who followed. Our good friend Betty helped with all our parties, bringing chips and dips and cheese balls and punch, setting out the food in her own Langeberger baskets and blue pottery. Betty loved us, helped us, and was always loyal to us.

Inside the house, I displayed posters showing the lives of the boys in pictures and hung their artwork on the walls. We filled tables full with Aaron and Joe's awards.

That summer before he started college, Joe worked with a steel construction crew. I said, "You aren't doing anything dangerous, are you? You're not climbing around on roofs?"

He assured me he was fine.

I later found out he had walked on steel beams high in the air.

Joe's dream was to be an engineer. He was barely seventeen when he started school at Purdue University, and he graduated in five years through their co-op program, with a degree in mechanical engineering. He quietly achieved all of this, practically on his own, never asking for help.

Although the doctors had said that Daddy's leukemia wasn't serious, they were wrong. About a year after his diagnosis, he began to need blood transfusions to replenish his platelets. Mick and Jo were pressed into service, taking Daddy to doctor appointments, taking him to the hospital, and helping to buy his medicine. Eventually the doctors sent him to Methodist Hospital in Indianapolis for chemotherapy, and I visited him there on the sixth floor. I drove him back home from Indianapolis, almost as if he were the child sitting beside me in the car and I was the parent. He wore his usual outfit: brown corduroy pants, earth-tone shirts, and a black leather vest that Elaine and Riley had bought him in South Dakota. He wore a hat over his long curly hair, which was now mostly gray.

Finally, after another trip to the hospital, they sent him home saying that no more could be done. They gave us a pill that would keep him from bleeding to death, but that pill in itself would cause him to die in a few days because it thickened his blood. Either way we knew he only had a few days left to live.

What a strange feeling it was to know when someone would die. But Daddy was ready. He talked about his death and planned his funeral like he was talking about going to the store. He told me to sell the house and how I should divide the money. He told me how to divide up the antiques and instructed me to sell the box full of old tools he had polished. He said he wanted everything at the funeral done the same way we had done for Mom.

We had visited him in his home a few weeks earlier and had talked about his future. At that time, I had felt like it was time to talk to him about eternity. He knew what Mom and all the rest of us believed. He had heard Billy Graham on TV. Throughout the years, whenever a Billy Graham crusade had come on, he had listened, but he would soon get fidgety and get up to make a sandwich in the kitchen. He knew what it was about, but he didn't want to face it.

There in the living room I brought up the fact that Mom was in heaven. I said, "I'd like to know you'll be going to heaven, too, along with all the rest of us. What's keeping you from becoming a Christian?"

He said, "Nothing, I guess."

I led him in a prayer of repentance to receive Jesus as his Savior. He was serious about it and was born again that day.

Now it was two weeks later, and we knew he had only a few days left. He talked to Mindy and me and Jeff, probably as much as he ever had at one time. Normally he didn't have much to say and would answer questions with only a word or two.

"What're you making, Don?"

"A fence."

"For back in the pasture?"

"Yep."

But not this time. He told us stories from World War II. He laughed and told us about going into the basements of German homes and drinking their wine, about turning his head when someone called out the name Gerhardt, about leading the mule trains in Panama. It was a special time together.

We slept there in the house and waited. Daddy was a thin shell of what he used to be, a slim mound under the gray wool blanket Mom had bought for him a few years before.

As the end came, we were all there in the room with him—Mindy, Jeff, Mick, Jo Etta, and me. I held his big, square hand in mine. His rough breathing shook him as if he were rumbling down railroad tracks on a train, mumbling about scenes from his life as if they were passing by.

He said, "I'm gonna need my lunch bucket," like he was getting ready to go to work. I remembered all the years that Mom had packed his lunch with sandwiches, little containers of fruit and cookies, and his silver thermos of coffee or milk. And he always brought back a little something that he didn't eat.

Finally the rumbling slowed down and stopped. Daddy died on October 18, 1995. The weather was warm for that time of year. I went outside and shot some baskets at the basketball hoop he had nailed onto the end of his garage for all the grandkids. The whole side of his garage was covered with round pebbly mud marks and hand prints. An IU symbol was on one side of the basket, and a Purdue symbol was on the other side.

It was nighttime and windy. The hillside was covered with oak trees whose leaves turn brown in the fall and hang on all winter. The leaves swished in the wind. Whenever I remember that home now, I picture it in the fall, in shades of brown—brown leaves, brown mud, brown trim on the house, brown tree trunks.

Daddy was buried in his brown corduroys and his black leather vest. We did everything the same as we did at Mom's funeral, except a friend from church played taps and the casket was draped in a military flag. I cried when they folded the flag into a triangle and presented it to me.

The patriarch of the family, as Mom had once called him, was gone. Mindy's and my childhood home was gone.

We went through the house. Mick and Elaine chose some items to keep that were meaningful to them, and Mindy and I divided up the rest. We looked at the antique tools that Daddy had carefully restored and polished.

Mindy said, "We can't sell these."

I agreed. "We'll keep them because they represent Daddy's life as a carpenter and a lover of antiques." We still have the antique tools in our homes.

RENEE

"I was going to go to Vienna this weekend, but instead I'm going to Cologne."
"This is me and my coworkers in London over New Year's."
"Here I am in Pisa in front of the Leaning Tower. I want to go to Rome before I come back home."

Renee was a world traveler, barely out of college, writing e-mails to us from Europe. She had done so well working for the Eli Lilly Company that they had sent her to live and work in Europe.

It wasn't the first time she'd been overseas. As early as eighth grade, she had traveled with us to Israel where we walked together in old Jerusalem, visited Masada, and learned about the ancient holy sites from our Jewish guide. It was the best field trip ever. Everything was full of significance because it was the land of the Bible and because Renee and I had read about Israel becoming a state in 1948 in *The Zion Chronicles.*

As a little girl, Renee was happy and compliant, playing with her little sister just as I had played with Mindy. Her first drawings of people were typical, with arms and legs coming right out of their heads. Her people looked like spiders floating in the air. She learned to read but had trouble with spelling—at first. But as she grew older, we could tell she was talented. She was diligent about her schoolwork, getting all As. She easily learned how to play the piano, while I struggled and never did catch on. She could listen to a song and then play it by ear.

Renee was a leader. People came to her for advice. She was the vice-president of her student council. She earned money working in the office of a beauty salon when she was only sixteen. She always had boyfriends.

Everything seemed to go well for her. Everything seemed under control. It was easy to overlook this child who never seemed to need anything, because there was always a crisis somewhere else to deal with, always babies and toddlers, always someone who was more demanding. So I didn't realize how much she was hurting inside and needed my attention.

Renee graduated as the valedictorian of her class, in a tie with two other girls. She was every bit as smart and competitive as her older brothers. She especially clashed with her brother Aaron because they shared the same driving ambition to excel. She was not about to let a boy be better than her, and Aaron was not about to be beaten by a younger sister. They were too much alike to appreciate each other.

Renee got a full scholarship to Depauw University, where she majored in physics and became the president of her sorority. After graduation, Eli Lilly snapped her right up to work for them. They sent her on some trips to Mexico during her first year and then began promoting her right and left. After just two years, she was sent to Germany, integrating new computer software for the company, with a sporty car and a nice German apartment included in the deal. She was also able to travel around Europe on the side.

Renee said, "I love it. I love working with people from all over the world. But after a while, a job is still a job you go to every day, even if it is in Europe."

She lived in Germany as long as Andy lived in Russia.

When Renee was a senior in high school, Audrey started first grade. All the kids were in school, finally. I wanted to get a part-time job, but I didn't have any marketable skills. I knew nothing about the computer Jeff had in his office. When I was in college, computers were as big as a room and only available to a few people. I hated feeling left out, so I decided to take a computer class. First I practiced typing, using a Gregg typing textbook from the library, and then I took *Introduction to Computers*, going to class once a week at IVY Tech. I loved going back to school and looked forward to my class all week.

I applied for a job at the library, listing my experience of raising children and speaking to the women at church. I said I loved to read. But they didn't hire me, even though I applied twice.

I then turned to the Eastern Hancock School District, which took me on as an elementary substitute teacher. I liked the schoolwork, I liked using the blackboard and sitting behind the desk, but I didn't like dealing with the kids. I was almost in tears sometimes because they wouldn't obey me, not even the kindergarteners. All of my time was spent keeping order, getting the kids to be quiet, and settling arguments. It was no different than being at home, no different than being a mom. The kids with ADHD totally frustrated me.

I also substituted in the cafeteria, but that was like working at home, too—feeding lots of kids and cleaning the kitchen.

But then my big break finally came. After adding more computer courses to my résumé and adding my experience at the school, I was hired by Dr. Weiss, a chiropractor in Greenfield.

Dr. Weiss looked like John Denver, only older. Once, when he went to a John Denver concert, he told them he was John's brother, and they believed him.

He was close to seventy years old, but he didn't know when to quit, even though he saw only a few patients a week. It was a good place to start learning about insurance and the medical field, though, since the pace was so slow. The doctor would come and go, leaving me alone for long periods of time. When he was there, he would talk to me about politics and religion.

Because I was the only employee, I did everything in the office. I handled the charts, the scheduling, the phones, and the billing. I put patients on the treatment tables, put hot packs on their backs, and explained subluxation of the vertebrae using a plastic model of the spine, even though I didn't really know what I was talking about. I cleaned the office, helped Dr. Weiss drag the Christmas tree up from the basement, and held up boards for him so he could repair the back porch on his house. After a while I decided that I wanted to find a real office job. It was just too weird working for Dr. Weiss.

I got a real job with Dr. Needham, a dermatologist in Greenfield with a busy and *normal* medical practice. I worked with Tisa, the office manager, who taught me everything about insurance and billing and transcription and so forth. It was a full-time job at a busy office. I had to do more than one task at the same time, but I already knew how to do that from life at home with the kids. I only worked there about a year because we were soon to move away from Greenfield.

VICKI

*"I'm not sure if we can give Vicki credit for these classes.
She has missed too many days of school."*

It was the end of Vicki's junior year. I explained to the assistant principal that if Vicki didn't get credit for these classes, she would probably be so discouraged that she would just quit school.

Going over the head of the assistant, I appealed to the principal, arguing that one of the absences was actually based on a technicality. He agreed, and Vicki got the credits she needed. A year later, Vicki graduated from high school with the vocational training to be a dental assistant. We made a big sign for the garage door at her graduation: "You made it through, Tissie Too!" It was a happy day for her. She had not liked going to school and just wanted to get away from home. She was spending most of her time in Indianapolis with friends.

Vicki was a sweet girl, thoughtful and sensitive. She stood out in a crowd with her thick, straight red hair—a nice sandy shade of red. But she didn't want red hair. Beginning in high school, she highlighted it to make it blonder. She said that someone complimented her wondrous hair almost every day. Pulled back, it was as heavy as a literal pony's tail.

But it seemed that Vicki had a lot of things to overcome. Aside from being born premature, being a middle child, coming so soon after Renee, and so forth, she seemed to get sick easily and had allergies. She broke her ankle sledding, she had an accident in Andy's car that caused the air bag to blow up in her face, and she hit a deer one night in her car. She said she didn't feel like she fit in with the other kids at school. Sometimes she even said she didn't fit in with our family. She even said that she was adopted. (But if she took a good look at the family, it was clear she was one of us.)

Not that everyone else didn't have things to overcome. That's just life. As the old saying goes, "Life is just one darn thing after another."

But there was more. When Vicki and Renee were teenagers, and even before that time, I depended on them as my oldest girls to help with the kids and the housework. I often called on Vicki to watch the little kids for me. She didn't mind at first. She liked learning how to cook and didn't mind watching her brothers or sisters once in a while. But sometimes it became too much.

One day as I was giving out orders to the girls, standing by the dishwasher with kids under my feet, it hit me. There was pain on Renee's face after I told her to do something, and it struck me how all of my conversations with the girls were based on either orders or reprimands. I wasn't talking to them about fun things or mother-daughter things. I did, of course, but not nearly enough for a daughter to feel loved and appreciated. I was at home with my children all the time, all of those years, day and night, but I still lacked a good mother-daughter connection with Renee or Vicki.

Some mothers and daughters connect by shopping together, but we didn't usually have fun on mother-daughter shopping trips. I didn't like to shop, and it was hard to find clothes that fit and were the right price. I remembered that these were the same problems Mindy and I had shopping with our mom. It was especially hard when the girls were too big for kids' clothes, but not old enough for the adult sizes.

I would pick out an item, hoping to speed things up. "How about this shirt?"

They'd say, "I'd never wear that. It looks too old lady-ish. I like this one."

I'd say, "It's too short." Or, "too tight." Or, "not on sale."

I would sometimes embarrass the girls, saying a little too loudly, "I can't find a size fourteen. This is the biggest they have."

Renee and I discussed our mother-daughter relationship years later when we visited her for a week in Germany. She had bought our plane tickets so we could see where she lived and how she worked for Eli Lilly there. She explained that she hadn't felt as if she'd had a loving mommy when she was growing up. She and Vicki remembered one time when we'd had a silly tea party. It stood out in their minds because it only happened once. It hurt me to think they felt this way. I knew she was right, but I explained how I had given my whole life, everything I had, for them.

I told her it was kind of like the song, "The Greatest Man I Never Knew," by Reba McIntire. Reba sings that she never really knew her dad because he was always so busy, always working. She says, "Everything he gave to us took all he had." Reba didn't realize how much her dad loved her because "he never said 'I love you.' Guess he thought I knew." Renee had played this song on the piano as a teenager, and I cried every time I read the words because it reminded me of my own dad. I told my kids I loved them, but like my dad, everything I gave took all I had.

Those years were hard for Vicki and Renee because of some of our convictions. I had been wearing only skirts and dresses, never jeans or shorts, since shortly after Andy was born. I agreed with the church's position that men should be masculine and women should be feminine. I had been such a tomboy, wearing my jeans and flannel shirts, that it was good for me to get into skirts and dresses for a change. It might have helped me change my outlook, but it was too much to impose on young girls in middle school and high school. They were embarrassed having to wear denim skirts and culottes year round in middle school. They didn't want to be different.

As Christian parents, we had set high standards for our girls. As preacher's kids, people expected them to measure up, but the older they got, the harder it was for them to conform. Even worse, families would come and go at the church, taking their teenagers with them, so sometimes the girls lost their best friends.

Renee and Vicki both rebelled; they just handled it differently. Renee became independent and self-confident, not wanting anybody's help. Vicki was more sensitive and insecure, looking outside our home for help and attention. She said that she just wanted to get away.

The boys had issues, too. Having to adjust to public school after being in home school for several years was hard for the boys, especially since we put them in during middle school, the most awkward time.

Sports caused the biggest problem for them. Because Jeff knew how sports could dominate a person's life, as it had in his family, he didn't want it to take over our boys' lives. Sports had become a "god" to him, and he wanted to make sure that God was in first place in our children's lives. But it was too strong of a conviction to place on the boys. School sports would have been healthy for them. All of the boys would have been good at basketball or football or any sport they would have tried. I'm sure we would have had a string of Barnett athletes, but when we finally let them play, it was too late. They each got a chance at playing a sport, but as juniors or seniors, it was too late for them to find a place on a team and do well when all the other kids had been playing together for years. Out of the older boys, Joe was the only one to play varsity basketball. It was his senior year. He sat on the bench and scored seven points all season.

At the same time, with the size of our family, it would have been almost impossible to drive to all the practices and games, especially because we lived several miles from the school. We would have been quite a sight, coming in with a row full of toddlers and babies to a basketball game. In fact, the boys would probably have been embarrassed to have us all file into the gym. Except for Andy, who was always proud of our large family, most of the kids liked us to enter the school in small groups so that people wouldn't see that we were all together. They just didn't want to be different, and a family of ten was different.

We had only the best intentions in all that we did. I read books on how to raise children, how to discipline, how to love. I tried to be fair and set up guidelines. I wanted to multiply my love. I wanted my family to grow up with the same values I had. But some of the restrictions were just too much for them to take. Even when we might have liked to lower our standards, it was almost impossible because of Jeff's position as a pastor in the church. Everything he taught was recorded on tape. And everyone watched the pastor's kids to see what they would do, to see if they would live up to what their dad had preached.

CHAPTER 11

DANNY

"I'm not gonna play football..."
"I'm a Christian, please pray for me..."
"I didn't do it..."
"I'm just going out with my buddies..."
"I'm gonna join the Navy..."
"I'm not graduating from high school, Mom..."
"Mom, I'm gonna be a rock star..."
"I just like literature, art, and music."

Danny was like a feather falling through the air, carried one way by the wind, then another, whichever way the wind would blow. Danny was a middle child like Vicki, often lost in the shuffle.

We made two big moves when Danny was in high school, taking him away from his friends in Eastern Hancock by moving to Indianapolis, then one year later moving to Pennsylvania. We didn't purposely try to upset our kids' lives, but these decisions to move were step by step breaking the hold of the past and bringing us into more freedom in our Christianity.

The church near Acton had suffered, not only from division, but also from an arson fire, set off by a teenager in the church. After much labor and money, the people rebuilt the church themselves, but it was still much like a military bunker. It had no room for teen or children's classrooms, rooms we now realized we needed to meet the needs of the whole congregation and to help move us out of our rut.

Our kids had never had separate classes for them. They always stayed in the main meeting with the adults. They listened and absorbed some of the teaching, but they also did creative things like keep track of how many times their dad said a certain word or phrase.

"Dad, you said the word *beloved* thirty-six times in the sermon today."

Our building was inadequate. We needed some drastic changes, and we were still resisted by people who wanted to keep things the way they were.

One day we ate lunch with Pastors Ken and Patti Troutman, who had visited our church a few times and knew of our spiritual background. We told them of the struggles we were having with our building and how the people were tired of working on it.

Patti said, "Why don't you just merge with our church?"

We laughed. "That would never work. Our people wouldn't go for it."

But it got us thinking. Even though it seemed impossible, how wonderful it would be to share leadership with a progressive church in a functional building, at the same time putting some distance between ourselves and the past. We never wanted to leave the Christian foundation we had laid at Faith Assembly; we just wanted to leave behind the extremes. It had been Christianity with knives sticking out of it, and it was hurting people.

The more we thought about it, the more we became fascinated with the idea of merging. We decided to just do it and let the chips fall where they would. We were dying the way we were.

Some of our members were upset or didn't like the way we handled the situation. Some tried the new merged church, re-named Christian Faith Center, and then left. But some stayed. This bold move and our new friendship with the Troutmans helped set us free some more.

After three years of driving to Indianapolis to the new church, Ken and Patti convinced us that we should move to Indianapo-lis. We loved our brick ranch home in the country, geese flying in overhead, moon shining on the water, country roads to walk down, but we decided to make the move. We bought a house in the eastside suburbs, where all the houses were made from the same three or four floor plans. Who would have ever thought I'd be living in Indianapolis?

So we got ready to move again. We were about in line with the national average of families moving every five years. But it wasn't so bad. How else do people sort out the garage and clean behind the refrigerator?

Mindy and I continued to stay in touch, even though we lived two hours apart. Sometimes we would each drive halfway and meet in Elwood to talk. There was always so much to say to bring each other up to date. After all, we did have twenty-one kids between us since Mindy had remarried and had an eleventh child, Nyla. Sometimes we would talk at the same time, and we laughed till we cried. In just a few minutes we'd be home again, we'd be kids again. Anyone standing nearby wouldn't understand what was so funny, but we had a history as sisters. You're never far from home when you're with family.

Mindy and I would talk about the past and also the present, where her problems continued. After she remarried, she found out that her new husband had a drinking problem. She explained situations to me that were big enough to overwhelm most people, but she would always be cheerful and see better times just around the corner.

Back to Danny. Danny tried wrestling and football, but sports weren't the most important thing for him. He wore saggy pants and took up skateboarding, tearing up boards on the deck as he tried to ride the skateboard along any edges he could find.

After the move to Indianapolis, Danny ended up in a big-city school with several thousand students. He got a shiny blue car and was always out with his buddies. I remembered when he had been such a happy little kid with his beautiful smile, perfect teeth, and classic good looks. He'd had a sense of humor that could make us all laugh. But now when he was around he didn't have much to say. He was getting into trouble. When I asked him about something, he always said he didn't do it. He had a way of talking his way out of anything. I was eager to believe the best, but eventually I questioned almost everything he said. Then he said I didn't trust him; then I said he had broken the trust; and on and on it went.

He was drifting along, not seeming to care about his future. Although he had made a serious commitment to be a Christian at a youth camp, he had trouble living it out. When a recruiter talked to him about joining the Navy, he decided that was the answer. He thought the discipline would be good for him. That was his plan until we decided to move to Pennsylvania.

SCOTT

"I'm not moving to Pennsylvania. I'll live with Joe and he can adopt me."

We had lived in our suburban home on Jay Drive for only one year when we were invited by Apostle Chuck Clayton to pastor a church in Pennsylvania. The idea seemed ridiculous because we had never considered leaving Indiana and our family. I was content in Indianapolis, although I thought the east side was ugly with its convenience stores and strip malls. In the background was the constant hum of the interstate.

I missed the country. I missed the stars at night. I missed the sound of frogs and crickets. But there was convenience: Restaurants, the mall, and grocery stores were all within a mile of our house. The church was not far away. The kids liked their new schools and being close to church friends. I never would have thought I could live in the city, but it had become our home.

Our house in the suburbs was a tri-level with plenty of room for our small family of just five kids still at home. The middle level contained our kitchen, dining room, and living room. Up a few stairs were several bedrooms, including the master bedroom. Down a few steps were the boy's bedroom and a family room with sectional couch, TV, and computer. It was a nice arrangement.

We liked to take walks around our suburban neighborhood, although the first time we tried, we got lost because of all the winding roads: Jay Drive, Jay Court, Andy Drive, Andy Court. We liked to identify the three or four different house designs and see how people had added different siding, porches, or landscaping so that all the houses looked a little different. That was the only interesting thing to do in our neighborhood.

We had gone through two Ford Econoline vans by this time and had finally scaled down to a red Dodge minivan. We soon got rid of the minivan and bought a red Ford Taurus and a cranberry Neon. No more vans for us! At least we never had to drive an extended fifteen-passenger van and look like people going on a field trip all the time.

Jeff took good care of his vehicles, getting the oil changed, washing the outside, cleaning up the trash. It was hard with the kids always leaving food wrappers, toys, and odd items behind them. One time we found enough change to take all the kids swimming by looking in all the cracks and crevices of the van.

Jeff tried to protect his vehicles, but the kids tended to scratch the van doors with bicycle handles or put dents in the hood with basketballs. Our beginning drivers were a little rough on the vehicles. As soon as we got the Neon, someone dented and scratched it on both sides. Rearview mirrors have been torn off, but no one has ever been hurt in a car, and that's all that really matters.

Apostle Chuck offered Jeff the church in Pennsylvania and tried to make it sound appealing. He described Titusville to us: "It's famous because the first oil well was drilled there— Drake's well. It's a quaint little town with Victorian homes and brick streets."

We actually had three options where Jeff could pastor, besides staying where we were. There was the church in Pennsylvania, Apostle Chuck's church in southern Indiana, or a new church in northern Indiana with some of our old Faith Assembly friends. We considered all three, actually listing on paper all the pros and cons of each, and prayed about what God wanted us to do.

I traveled with Jeff to the church in Titusville, thinking I could rule it out as a possibility after I saw it. Instead, after meeting the people and worshiping with them, I was overwhelmed that they were asking us to be their leaders. The people were talented and friendly—small-town people, country people, and businessmen. It would be a fresh start for us. No one would be quoting past tapes or old doctrines to us. We decided to move there. A motivational saying on a calendar encouraged us: "The biggest regrets in life are the opportunities not taken." We didn't want any regrets.

We found a house on Walnut Street in Titusville, a two-story house with light-blue siding, very old but already remodeled. We could move right in. It was four rooms deep, both up and downstairs. We even had a pool and a lot that went all the way back to the alley. And the price was right. Compared to our house in Indianapolis, we were getting a real bargain.

But Danny said he was not moving. We told Danny he could move to Las Vegas, live with Aaron, and finish his senior year there. Aaron's ambition would be a good influence on him, we thought. Danny agreed and forgot his plans to join the Navy.

Scotty didn't want to move, either. He was only seventeen at the time, a junior in high school. We made the difficult decision to have our son Joe become Scotty's legal guardian so that he could finish his last two years of high school in Indiana. They lived in Columbus and drove to Indianapolis every week to be part of the church and youth group where Joe was a leader.

Scotty found out that this arrangement was harder than he had expected. He had to grow up fast. He worked part time, he felt alone in his new school, and he had to fend for himself much of the time because Joe didn't baby him. But he did it. He even graduated from Columbus High School a semester early and then started college at the Indiana University-Purdue University campus in Indianapolis.

We missed Scotty a lot. We missed two important years of his life when he should have been at home with us. As a little boy, Scotty had been headstrong at times, not wanting to stay in his crib, fighting with Danny, threatening to run away from home. But he outgrew that. Scott is a pleasure to be around. He is the life of the party, full of love and humor. He can always make us laugh even though he likes to test the very limits of what is decent and right.

Meanwhile, we liked living in Titusville. As a small college town with shady streets, it reminded us of North Manchester. For Jeff, it was wonderful to work with people who had never heard of Dr. Freeman or what he taught. We made new friends. We saw a successful youth center open in the church, something the church had wanted for years. We saw a Walmart come to Titusville, something the town had wanted for years.

Soon after we moved, I started working for an orthopedic surgeon as a front-office secretary, and later became a transcriptionist at Carter Orthopedics, where they make prosthetic legs and all kinds of bracing and shoe inserts. I typed all day, answered phones, and scheduled appointments. It was only half a mile from home, so I could walk to work. It was practically across the street from the church. We had never lived in a place where school, work, church, and home were so close to each other.

BRYCE

"Why did you make me move to Pennsylvania?"

Bryce was only fifteen at the time, so naturally he moved with us to Titusville. After living in the city, it was hard for him to make the change to this small town. He adjusted and made some friends, but he kept looking back to Indiana like it was the Promised Land.

We reminded Bryce that being one of the youngest in the family, he was allowed to do things the older boys hadn't done. He had lots of clothes. We handed him so much money that we called him the "black hole." Money just disappeared from his hands. The older boys had always had to work for their money. Bryce just said, "At least they got to live in Indiana."

Bryce was our baby boy. We had called him "Little Bubs." He was the cute little brother—so cute when he used to play with his farm set and John Deere tractors. So cute when he made forts and trails. So cute when he wanted a rope for his birthday for climbing trees and inventing. But Bryce grew up. He became tall, with a strong arm for football and graceful moves for basketball.

If any one of our children would be able to do well in school sports, it would be Bryce. He had played basketball and football in middle school and had played for an AAU basketball team in Indiana. With this experience going into his freshman year in this small town, he would surely shine. We were from Indiana after all. We knew about basketball. All the boys had grown up playing ball with each other and with friends at the Greenfield Park. When Michael Jordan became famous, the boys were just the right age to make him their hero. They wore Bulls coats and shirts and Jordan tennis shoes. They lowered the basketball goal so they could dunk.

But Titusville didn't seem to care about basketball. There were no large gyms, no basketball hysteria. Bryce played well anyway, and he was voted most valuable player his senior year, but he was disappointed with the program all four years. He didn't get along with the coach, and the Titusville Rockets never had a winning season or even made it to the playoffs.

"If only I could have stayed in Indiana," Bryce said. "If only we could have had a different coach."

The older boys said, "If only we could have had the chance to play ball like Bryce. If only we'd had all the clothes Bryce has."

Andy said, "If only someone would have made me go to college."

Aaron said, "If only we wouldn't have had to be home schooled."

The older girls said, "If only we could have worn normal clothes."

All the kids said, "If only Dad would have played professional football," and, "If only we were rich."

"Enough!" I said. "If Dad had played professional football, you probably wouldn't even be here. No more 'what if's!"

Pennsylvania did have football hysteria. Every Friday night, the entire town of Titusville migrated to the end of town, past the fifteen-foot-long actual rocket, into the football field by the abandoned Cytemp steel mill. Northwest Pennsylvania loved football, and they loved the Pittsburgh Steelers.

Bryce tried out for football his senior year, even though he hadn't played with the team before. Jeff was one of the assistant football coaches, so it was going to be fun. If only Bryce hadn't hurt his thumb on the first day of practice, he would surely have been a good quarterback. He had to have surgery and couldn't play the rest of the season, so that was that.

Bryce graduated from high school and immediately moved back to Indiana. And just a few months later, he moved to Las Vegas.

RACHELLE

"I'm going to the 2004 Olympics."

Rachelle started out with bowed legs and a foot that turned in. At the Yogi Bear Campground where I took the kids to swim, someone had once said, "Look at that cute little bowlegged baby!" I didn't think it was so cute. We prayed for her legs to straighten out, and as she grew older, they did. She has become a beautiful young lady with a quiet personality and a wide smile of perfect teeth, one of the few in the family who didn't need braces.

Rachelle loved to run and jump and tumble. We watched the video of the 1984 Olympics until we knew it backwards and forwards, especially the gymnastics. Rachelle watched Mary Lou Retton and said, "I want to take gymnastics lessons and go to the 2004 Olympics when I'm sixteen."

She practiced in the front yard doing flips and cartwheels. She did get to take some gymnastics lessons in Greenfield at the same gym where Jaycee Phelps had trained to go to the 1996 Olympics. I didn't want to crush her hopes, but I explained that someone couldn't go to the Olympics unless it became the single goal of the entire family, starting when the child was about age two. It was already too late for that.

But the gymnastics practices helped later when she became a cheerleader in Titusville. She got everyone's attention doing backflips along the edge of the gym floor. Her flips were sometimes better than the actual game.

Rachelle also found out that she was good at the shot put and discus throws. At one track meet in middle school, she actually took first place in four different events! She was afraid that weightlifting would give her a tankish figure, but she didn't need to worry about that.

Rachelle has always loved art. All of my kids have been able to produce a good drawing in school, and I have a whole cupboard full of ceramics projects, but Rachelle has had the greatest passion for art. Her very first acrylic painting of tulips, painted from a picture the size of a match box, is still framed in our dining room. She has an entire portfolio of artwork now, in acrylics, watercolors, and pastels.

Rachelle begged me to let her paint her bedroom until I finally gave in. Two of her walls are now Pepto-Bismol pink, and one is bright orange, with a pink, orange, and purple mural in the style of Van Gogh's *Starry Night* on the other wall. I have to admit, with her coordinating curtains and accessories, her room looks very nice.

Rachelle missed Indianapolis just like Bryce did. She loved that one year we had lived in the city. She loved going to a school with thousands of kids from all races. There's very little diversity in Titusville, and she hates prejudice.

Each year we make three or four trips back to Indiana to see our family, especially at Thanksgiving and Christmas. We had started celebrating Christmas several years earlier when we lived in the brick ranch by Greenfield because we realized it was doing more harm than good to ignore this holiday. We believed that we could bring glory to God in it. We started developing our own family Christmas traditions, beginning with lights and decorations, presents, and food. We tried to get as much of the family together as we could to celebrate, usually in Indianapolis.

I told the kids we would try not to focus so much on expensive gifts but on meaningful things at Christmas. Each year I gave them framed family pictures or collages of their baby pictures to put in their own homes.

Then I came up with an activity called Memory Bowl. I wrote words on little strips of paper like *cat, Greenfield, bicycle, Eastern Hancock, the McNeils, sandbox,* and so on, to stimulate our memories and bring out family stories. One at a time, each person drew a word, recounted the first memory that came to mind, and then everyone was free to add their own memories, as well. It worked perfectly. People were jumping up and talking at the same time. We found out things we never knew before, like who had really written the bad words on Ms. Snipe's shed and who had really wrecked David's moped. We found out where the kids really were when we thought they were playing basketball at the park or when we thought they were asleep in bed. It had been so long since these things happened that no one got in trouble. The kids remembered how their Grandpa Gearhart backed over their bicycles with his truck. The boys remembered how they had dragged home a frozen beaver and Bryce wanted to skin it with a kitchen knife and sell the fur. We all laughed until we cried. I loved seeing the kids all together, reliving and preserving our family history.

You're never far from home when you're with family.

AUDREY

"Mom and Dad, just don't ever look or smell like old people."

Audrey is bold and talkative. Sometimes it gets her in trouble in school, but she is not afraid to talk to adults, to ask someone for help, or to give a report in front of the class. She can persuade people to buy candy bars for fundraisers and get kids to come to the youth center.

Sometimes she thinks she doesn't have any special talents when she hears us talk to people about Rachelle's artwork or gymnastics.

"I don't have any talents," she says.

"Yes, you do. Someday you'll be the mayor," I said. "You'll be a leader."

Audrey will always be the baby of the family. Sometimes she's glad about it and sometimes she's not. She knows she's gotten more attention than the older kids. As a freshman in high school, she has more freedom and spends more time with her friends than all her brothers and sisters ever did. Our standards have relaxed. Mom and Dad have mellowed, for better or worse.

But Audrey also realizes that I'm older than most of her friends' moms. I saw a stroller in the antique store just like the one I sat in as a baby. I don't like running around or going shopping. I like to stay home. She watches her mom and dad getting older, and she doesn't like it.

She said, "Don't dress like old people. And I don't want to come back to your house after I leave and have it smell like old people!"

I said, "We'll do our best."

I don't feel old—not inside. In fact, sometimes in a crowd I still feel like that awkward girl in junior high so long ago. But now, with just two kids at home, Jeff and I are beginning to look forward to the empty nest. It feels as though the grace God had given me for raising my family is beginning to wear off. We've got grandkids now. We're saving money for retirement. Our home life has changed.

These days, Jeff leaves the church at five o'clock to pick me up at Carter Orthopedics after work. We go home, I fix a thirty-minute meal, we fill our plates from off the stove, and we eat supper sitting on the couch, watching the news or *Home Improvement* reruns. Sometimes the girls eat with us, but usually not. The days when we all sat around a ten-foot table and went through twelve gallons of milk a week are a distant memory.

But our lives still center around Jesus and the church. Jeff is still the pastor, and I'm still his encouragement. We're still at church every Sunday and several times a week. We still travel to meetings and believe something good is just about to happen.

As we travel, I tell Jeff, "If it wasn't for you, I wouldn't have seen other countries and been to the four corners of the United States. We've traveled from San Francisco to Boston to New Orleans to Milwaukee for your meetings. And I was able to go along for free."

When we walk into a room, anywhere, people still turn to look at Jeff because he is such a striking figure, whether in his preacher's suit or his Titusville Rockets football shirt. I tell him,

"If it wasn't for you, people wouldn't even notice me in a crowd. People know me because of you. I'd just be a flower on the wallpaper."

We both say, "If it wasn't for you, I wouldn't have these ten children!"

For a long time, I've seen my family in myself. I see my mother in my own round face and the shape of my legs. I'm like her when I run in short bursts from the car to the house. When I'm quiet and hermitish, I'm my dad. I hear my sister's voice when I pronounce certain words.

Now I see myself in my kids—when they tell me of all the books they've read, when they tell me about a sunset or storm they saw, when they are quiet in a crowd, when they can't decide what to buy.

When the kids were little, I loved to see them all clean and dressed up for church, sitting in a row, Bibles and papers in hand, everything in order. After a chaotic week at home, everybody looked good. I was so proud of my family. They seemed to be turning out all right.

Now I see them grown up, in their own homes, starting their own families, with their own plans and ideas and success. I'm so proud of them. They are turning out all right. They each have their own file box of cards now, filling up with their own life's happenings and stories.

They see what I've written here and tell me what I've left out.

"Mom, I played tennis, too! I was number one my junior and senior year," said Bryce.

"What about when I hurt my shoulder?" asked Audrey.

"What about our trip to Mammoth Cave?" they ask.

I haven't even mentioned their boyfriends and girlfriends.

They'll just have to write their own books.

EPILOGUE

> *Home is the place where, when you have to go there, they have to take you in.*
>
> ROBERT FROST

Actually, home is where they always love you. No matter what. Not just because they have to.

My kids have a greater love and loyalty now for each other and for their mom and dad than they ever had when we were all living together. It seems to come with leaving home. They have helped each other out, they take each other in, and they travel great distances just to get together. They all help with the grandkids. Nothing makes a mother happier than seeing her family love each other like that.

Jeff is the patriarch, with a whole web of households growing under him.

Here is an update, a brief snapshot of our family.

Andy married Rebekah Weisjahn not long after coming back from Russia. They live in a new home outside of Indianapolis with their two sons, Alex and Zach, and their daughter, Alivia. Alex, our oldest grandchild, is starting first grade. Andy works at Federal Express and Integral, a company that makes security systems. He and Joe played in a band called Jacob's Patience for several years, and Andy still looks for opportunities to play drums in a Christian band. He plays on the Christian Faith Centre worship team. Rebekah is an artist and interior decorator.

Aaron and his wife, Stacy, live in Las Vegas where Aaron is a senior loan officer for Custom Home Loans and invests in real estate. Aaron worked for National Airlines as a dispatcher until the airlines went bankrupt after 9/11, and then he got involved in home refinancing and real estate, learning by experience and by reading many books. When his kidney transplant failed after five years, Renee, his sister and childhood rival, donated a kidney for a second transplant, which has been much more successful than the first. Stacy is from Greenfield, Indiana, but they met while they both worked for National Airlines. Aaron played bass for several years in a Las Vegas Band called Countersink, with his brother Danny on drums.

Joe married Rachel Wiesjahn, Rebekah's younger sister. Joe is a mechanical engineer and received his MBA at Indiana University. Rachel also graduated from Indiana University. They moved to Detroit, where Joe works for ArvinMeritor, a global manufacturing company that makes automotive parts. While he lived in Indiana, Joe played bass, and Rachel sang on the Christian Faith Centre worship team. Joe was also the assistant youth pastor at the church.

Renee lives in a condominium in downtown Indianapolis where she works at Eli Lilly Headquarters. She took a break from her job while still in Germany to donate a kidney to Aaron. She said, "Isn't that what anybody would do?" She has been promoted to team leader at Lilly's, overseeing the people she used to work with. She is preparing to get her MBA, and she likes to play her new piano.

Vicki and her son, Jae, live in Indianapolis. Vicki works as a dental assistant in a busy dental clinic. She has done a wonderful job making a home for herself and little Jae. She likes to travel to Las Vegas or Pennsylvania to see her family and plans to move to Las Vegas next spring. Vicki and Renee like to spend time together, eating out and playing pool, but they also like to do counted cross stitch at home.

Danny, Alana, and their son, Camren, live in Las Vegas, where Danny works as a server at Ventano's Italian Restaurante. He likes the restaurant business, but he also likes to read and has done some writing. Danny has found direction and purpose for his life, and he says he thinks of his mom and dad every day. It would be hard to find a prouder father than Danny (unless it would be Andy). Danny is a drummer and has played in Las Vegas bands.

Scott worked as a bank teller in Indianapolis while going to IUPUI. His coworkers and customers loved him, and he always balanced out at the end of the day. Now he lives in Las Vegas, working as a marketing representative for Custom Home Loans. He is halfway through college and plays the acoustic guitar.

Bryce also lives in Las Vegas. He is a loan processor, part of the Barnett team working together at Custom Home Loans. He will be starting college soon and would like to have his own business someday. He has to prove to his older brothers that he can be a success, too. When they're not working, the boys in Las Vegas go skiing, climb mountains, or just hang out together.

Rachelle is a senior at Titusville High School, a member of the National Honor Society. She was chosen to go the Pennsylvania Governor's School of the Arts, one of fifty selected from the state of Pennsylvania in the visual-arts category. She will have a head start toward college and a career in art.

Audrey is a sophomore in high school, a social butterfly, always with her friends. It's too early to tell what she will want to be when she grows up. Both Rachelle and Audrey sing on the youth worship team and like to dance. Audrey also writes poetry.

Jeff continued his schooling by correspondence and earned a bachelor of theology degree from Trinity College of the Bible. He hopes to eventually obtain a masters degree in pastoral ministry.

Years ago we bought an oil painting of a southern plantation with this scripture written on it: "His seed shall be mighty upon the earth: The generation of the upright shall be blessed. Wealth and riches shall be in his house: And his righteousness endures forever" (Psalm 112:2–3).

We bought this painting from Brad Thompson of New Orleans. At the time, we had just three little boys, but we said, as a confession of our faith, that our children would be mighty and that we would be blessed and have riches in our house. It has come true. God has blessed our home.

Someday we'll be finished with our work here in Titusville, and we'll be moving on. We'll be "Back Home Again in Indiana," or maybe somewhere else. But wherever we are, we'll be home. And if you were looking for heroes in this story, I hope you found them. They were there.

THE END

To order additional copies of
NEVER FAR FROM HOME
have your credit card ready and call
1 800-917-BOOK (2665)

or e-mail
orders@selahbooks.com

or order online at
www.selahbooks.com

Printed in the United States
37221LVS00004BA/148-177